Services *for the* urban poor

Services *for the* urban poor

3.

Action Planning Guidelines

Andrew Cotton & Kevin Tayler

Water, Engineering and Development Centre
Loughborough University
2000

Water, Engineering and Development Centre,
Loughborough University,
Leicestershire, LE11 3TU, UK

© A.P. Cotton and W.K. Tayler, 2000

ISBN 13 Paperback: 978 0 90605 580 9
ISBN Ebook: 9781788533454
Book DOI: http://dx.doi.org/10.3362/9781788533454

A catalogue record for this book is available from the British Library.

A reference copy of this publication is also available online at:
http://www.lboro.ac.uk/wedc/publications/sftup.htm

Cotton, A.P. and Tayler, W.K. (2000)
Services for the Urban Poor:
Section 3. Action Planning Guidelines
WEDC, Loughborough University, UK.

WEDC (The Water, Engineering and Development Centre) at Loughborough University in the UK is one of the world's leading institutions concerned with education, training, research and consultancy for the planning, provision and management of physical infrastructure for development in low- and middleincome countries.

This edition is reprinted and distributed by Practical Action Publishing.
Since 1974, Practical Action Publishing has published and disseminated books and information in support of international development work throughout the world. Practical Action Publishing trades only in support of its parent charity objectives and any profits are covenanted back to Practical Action (Charity Reg. No. 247257, Group VAT Registration No. 880 9924 76).

This document is an output from project R7292 funded by the UK Department for International Development (DFID) for the benefit of low-income countries. The views expressed are not necessarily those of DFID.

Acknowledgements

The financial support of the Department for International Development of the British Government is gratefully acknowledged. The authors would particularly like to thank their many urban engineering colleagues and friends throughout India, Pakistan and Sri Lanka with whom they have worked for the last fifteen years. Their experience has been central to the preparation of this work. Mr P Srinivasa Rao from Hyderabad, India provided a critical review of earlier drafts and additional material for Sections 4 and 6. Colleagues at WEDC and GHK Research and Training provided information and comments throughout the development of the work. We also acknowledge the inclusion of some material from earlier work jointly authored with Dr Richard Franceys. Finally, we wish to acknowledge Sue Cotton for her editorial contributions and the patience and skill of Rod Shaw and Glenda McMahon of the WEDC Publications Office in the design and production of the manual.

Contents

Section 3

Action Planning Guidelines

Who should read this
- Senior local officials at town/city level, including: programme directors; programme component managers who are responsible for developing and implementing action plans for improving services for the poor in towns and cities.
- Senior technical support staff on attachment to the programme including NGOs and local/international consultants.
- Managers of other concerned line departments and their staff.

Objectives of this section
To propose a framework for action planning to develop local neighbourhood plans and area service plans for networked infrastructure which focuses on the importance of linking these together through consensus building.

What this section tells you
The purpose of action planning is that it leads to **action** being taken which improves services for the urban poor.

The action planning process must **involve everybody who has influence** on what happens; local politicians can be of key importance.

Action planning is concerned with adopting a methodical approach to **find out what is already there** and to build on it.

The proposed **framework for action planning** has three components:
- developing Local Action Plans which respond to the demands and priorities of service users in urban poor areas (Section 3a);
- developing and coordinating Network Service Plans which deal with the supply of services from city-wide networks which is necessary to meet the local demand (Section 3b);

- bringing together the key people to adopt the Local Action Pans and Network Service Plans and agree a way forward which leads to implementation (Section 3c).

Support for the action planning process will be needed in two broad areas: firstly, developing participatory approaches; and secondly, institutional capacity building.

The **starting point** for action planning differs between neighbourhoods, user groups and communities, all of which are at different stages of development; action planning finds out and builds on what is already there.

The local context: where to use these Guidelines

These Guidelines for action planning make two very important assumptions:

- there is a commitment within municipal government to improve services for the poor which has higher level policy support from state/central government; and
- this policy supports a more decentralised approach to planning which accepts the importance of involving users in the process.

The extent to which these conditions exist is highly variable; yet without these 'policy drivers' it is very unlikely that the potential benefits from improved planning of services will be realised. The local institutional and political context is thus of central importance to what can be achieved.

There exist many situations in which a lot of preparatory work will be required in order to convince local officials firstly of the importance of involving users in local planning and secondly in developing a more integrated approach to city wide planning. This is beyond the scope of this manual and we make reference to other work which deals with these issues. These Guidelines for action planning are appropriate for situations where the above policy support is in place, including where there is external donor/lending agency support both for financing improvements and to provide technical assistance to local programme managers.

Basic principles

This section of the manual proposes a way of preparing Action Plans for improving services for the urban poor. The whole point of planning is that it leads to *action* being taken which improves services for the urban poor. Typically this is likely to include improvements to some or all of the following services:

- water supply;
- sanitation;
- drainage;
- access and paving;
- solid waste;
- power supply and security lighting; and
- community buildings.

The most effective way forward is to find out what is already there and investigate the best ways to improve services through better operation and maintenance of existing services and construction of new facilities. To do this successfully we must involve firstly the local people who are the users of the services, and secondly the officials of the municipality and other agencies who provide urban services. We are likely to need the help and support of others, such as local NGOs, consultants, and outside agencies in doing this.

Networked services require supporting infrastructure which is external to the household and neighbourhood. These can be classified into 'feeder' and 'collector' networks. Examples of feeder networks include :

- piped water supply; and
- power supply.

Examples of collector networks include:

- main drainage;
- solid waste collection; and
- sewered sanitation.

Non-networked services at the neighbourhood and household level can be developed independently of municipal services through local action alone; these include:

- wells and handpumps;
- unsewered sanitation;
- local drainage to soakpits or ponds; and
- solid waste disposal in pits.

An important lesson from past experience is that action planning has rarely been effective unless it involves everybody who has influence on what happens. Like it or not, this includes locally elected representatives. Councillors can be powerful supporters of plans for improving services; on the other hand, if they are excluded, they can be in a position to make matters difficult. Always remember that the existence of a plan does not mean that action will automatically follow; the role of local Programme Managers is to make sure that the plans are implemented and that *action* is taken. They need to mobilise all the support they can get in order to do this successfully.

We must also be realistic in our expectations of what can be achieved; it is very unlikely that all of the points in the proposed framework will be adopted. However, we can at least move some way to improving the prevailing situation by taking up what proves possible and workable in the local situation.

Framework for action planning

Two distinct types of plan need to be prepared and coordinated, one representing the demand and the other the supply. The Local Programme Director and Programme Sector Managers (for example, Engineering, Community Development, Health) have a crucially important role to play in making sure that these two types of plans are prepared and co-ordinated. Table 3.1 describes a framework for the action planning process which has three components.

Table 3.1. Action Planning Framework	
Component	**Description**
Local Action Plan	■ This is how the urban poor articulate their demand for improved services. ■ Local action planning finds out what services the users want and the extent to which they are prepared to allocate the resources at their disposal. ■ From this, full details of improvements to tertiary (neighbourhood) infrastructure are developed, including who pays for what.
Network Service Plan	**Area Network Service Plans** ■ This investigates how the networked infrastructure outside each neighbourhood can best supply services in order to match the demand which is expressed in the Local Plan.

Table 3.1. continued	
Component	**Description**
	■ Area Network Service Plans focus on the capacity of different parts of the secondary infrastructure networks, the demands which will be made, and on improvements to O&M and construction of new works. The Plans will also cover some parts of the primary networks. ■ The actual area covered by each Area Network Service Plan is determined by the 'command areas' of the existing networks. A good starting point is to use the area covered by the municipal Ward, as this often corresponds with the administrative unit for basic O&M services. Primary networks will extend beyond individual Wards, into Zones/Circles and to the town as a whole.
	Co-ordination of Area Network Service Plans ■ Area Network Service Plans need to be coordinated to ensure that the demands made on the primary networks which go beyond the limits of the individual area plans can be satisfied. This will be relatively simple for small towns but complicated for larger cities. ■ This co-ordination is best organised according to specific local institutional responsibilities: for example, there may be specialist line agencies for water and power, whilst the municipality deals with drainage and solid waste management. ■ The concerned institution is then responsible for developing town/city wide proposals for the necessary improvements to the primary networks.
Consensus building	■ This is the key to the planning process; it needs to involve: urban poor residents; officers of the municipality and specialist line agencies; and political representatives of the municipality. ■ It needs to bring together the Local Action Plans and Area Network Service Plans in a local forum where they are discussed, amended and agreed by all concerned. ■ This becomes the basis for action, for following up on progress, and ultimately for monitoring operation and maintenance. In this way, the new approaches can be institutionally learned and absorbed.

Support for action planning

Many of the activities which follow on from the framework in Table 3.1 require a lot of support. Throughout the whole process of planning and subsequent implementation, local Programme Mangers need to:

- define the support required;
- identify who can provide the support; and
- estimate and access the resources to fund the support.

Support will be needed in two broad areas.

- **Participatory approaches** to local action planning. See Tools 1, 2 and 3 which are associated with Section 3a of the manual; these will provide initial guidance on what needs to be done to prepare urban poor groups for local action planning and the potential support roles which NGOs can play.

- **Institutional capacity building** to support the more widespread adoption of innovative approaches within the lead agency. Table 2.2 in Section 2 of this manual can be used as a starting point to develop a capacity building agenda.

Where do we start from?

In practice it can take a long time to prepare the proposals for urban services improvement programmes. If the programme is funded by external donors or possibly national government it is highly likely that both national and international consultants will be involved. Project preparation involves initial survey work and discussions with the leaders and managers of local institutions and with some urban poor groups to build up an overview of the town or city and its problems. When the programme starts, we do have some information, although it will be of a very 'broad brush' nature. For example:

- urban poor areas to be targeted and their approximate population, identified on a city plan showing municipal Wards;

- some work using participatory techniques will probably have been done in a handful of urban poor areas; and

- an overview of city level infrastructure networks.

The key point here is that these initial studies will also reveal that different neighbourhoods, user groups and communities are at different stages of development, both in terms of the services available and the extent to which they are already mobilised for other activities through CBOs and NGOs. There is no common baseline; we do not actually start from 'zero', which is why the whole focus of the action planning process is to adopt a methodical approach to find out what is already there and to build on it.

Timing/phasing action planning activities

The purpose of the Area Network Service Plans and the co-ordinated plans for networked services at the town/city level is to ensure that the town infrastructure networks are able to support the networked service improvements at the tertiary level as expressed in the Local Action Plans.

This creates a problem with regard to the relative timing of these planning activities because, theoretically speaking, we do not know the demands on the city wide systems until the Local Action Plans are complete. This implies that the Area/Municipal level planning starts after the local action planning is complete. However, this is not workable, as planning and implementing improvements to primary and secondary infrastructure can be complicated, particularly when it involves coordinating and negotiating with several different agencies. We therefore need to work out a programme which coordinates the Local and Area Network Service Plans. Table 3.2 suggests how activities associated with each component of action planning could be phased.

Table 3.2. Phasing of action planning

Local action planning	Action Plans for Networked Services
Decide on the structure and process for consultation in local action planning *See Tool 2 Participatory information gathering*	Set up the structure for Consensus Building *See Section 3c Consensus Building*
Identify a small number of project areas which broadly represent the range of situations likely to be encountered across the city *See Tool 1 Preparing users and community groups for action planning*	Identify the relevant Wards and commence work: ■ establish contact ■ find out what is there ■ identify future plans *See Tool 11 Initial groundwork*
Start work at a pilot level developing Local Action Plans in these areas *See Tool 4 Initial survey and groundwork*	Analyse capacity of existing systems *See Tool 13 Assessing system capacity*
Determine the typical demands for: ■ water supply ■ power supply ■ drainage ■ solid waste management ■ sewerage *See Tool 7 User demand for service improvements; also* *See Tool 8 Gender issues* *See Tool 9 Formation of user groups*	Take these demands as inputs to assessing additional demand for the Area Network Service Plan ■ Assume they are typical for the city as a whole ■ Work out the additional demands across the city on this basis *See Tool 14 Preparing Area Network Service Plans*
Implement the Local Action Plans in the pilot areas; review any changes to the demands expressed in the Local Action Plan	Take note of any major changes to demand
Proceed with local action planning	Proceed with Area Network Service Plans and coordination of these across the town/city. Take note of any major changes to demand as local action planning moves ahead. Wherever possible incorporate changes as necessary.

How to use these guidelines

These guidelines cover the three parts of the action planning process described in Table 3.1 above and are structured as follows:

Section 3a: Preparing Local Action Plans: Framework and supporting tools.

Section 3b: Preparing Action Plans for Networked Services: Framework and supporting tools.

Section 3c: Consensus Building.

The framework is made up of a number of different components which address issues which are relevant to the plan; these are presented as a sequence of planning activities.

Associated with each component of the framework are one or more tools; these go into detail about what actually needs to be done with regard to each component of the framework, and hence to prepare the Action Plan.

Detailed technical issues about infrastructure planning for the different service sectors are dealt with in Section 4: Technical Guidelines.

Section 3a

Preparing Local Action Plans

Who should read this
- Senior local officials at town/city level, including: programme directors; programme component managers who are responsible for developing and implementing action plans for improving services for the poor in towns and cities.
- Senior technical support staff on attachment to the programme including NGOs and local/international consultants.
- Managers of other concerned line departments and their staff.

Objectives of this section
To propose a framework and supporting tools for local action planning which responds to the demands and priorities of service users in urban poor areas. This should be read in conjunction with Section 3b on network service planning and Section 3c on Consensus Building.

What this section tells you
A **framework for local action planning** is presented which comprises the following stages.
- Team building
- Establish contact
- Preparing users for action planning
- Find out what is already there
- Assess users priorities and demand
- Identify need for promotion activities
- Explore technical options
- Discuss operation & maintenance requirements
- Estimate indicative costs
- Review costs

- Reassess user priorities and demand
- Modify technical details
- Engineering design
- Cost recovery
- Implementation procedures
- Draw up Local Action Plan

Gender and **User groups** are two important cross cutting issues which need to be considered in each of the steps of the framework.

It is important to develop a simple, consistent **reporting format.**

The **fieldwork teams** have primary responsibility for preparing the plan and to make sure that the contents are agreed with the users.

The following **supporting tools** are provided

- Preparing users and community groups for action planning
- Participatory information gathering
- The role of NGOs
- Initial survey and groundwork
- User perceptions of existing services
- Technical options and levels of service
- User demand for service improvements
- Gender issues
- Formation of user groups
- Cost recovery

The need for local action planning

The purpose of the Local Action Plan is to find out what individual households, user groups and other community groups want individually and collectively, and what resources they themselves are willing to commit. The plan needs to reflect the priorities of residents for improved service delivery; not everyone has to have the same thing and we should avoid applying standard solutions to everybody.

Traditional approaches to planning which have been 'top down' have rarely if ever worked in relation to improving the situation of the urban poor because they ignore the concerns, priorities and activities of local people. The most important point is that the Local Action Plans need to be developed in a participatory way, which involves meeting regularly with groups of residents, finding out about their priorities and developing the plan with them so that it reflects what they actually want.

This approach may be very different from the routine way in which municipal officials are used to working, and it is very important that preparatory orientation and staff training is provided well before the action planning programme is due to start.

Framework for local action planning

Table 3a.1. presents the framework for local action planning as a series of steps to be followed; it gives a brief description of each component and refers to the various tools which describe the components in more detail, and provide help with what you actually need to do. The key point here is that all of the stages are developed in a participatory way, that is, through joint discussions, meetings and interviews which involve the programme team and the service users.

Note that we are not always talking about building new infrastructure; **improving operation and maintenance is the best way to improve services**. It is incorrect to jump to the conclusion that because something is not functioning properly there is automatically a need to build something new. It is therefore essential to have people with sound technical knowledge as part of all service planning activities.

Table 3a.1. Framework for local action planning

Activity	Brief description	Further guidance
Team building	Set up a system for managing the fieldwork. Field staff are crucial members of the programme who will be dealing directly with service users. Consider creating inter-disciplinary teams comprising: ■ engineering ■ community/social development ■ health ■ other sector specialists as required Define roles and responsibilities, reporting lines and arrange training in participatory methods and how Local Action Plans will be developed.	Tool 2 Participatory information gathering
Establish contact	Fieldwork teams make contact with ■ residents in the target areas; and ■ municipal Councillors. The first stage of establishing contact with urban poor communities is critically important and has to be handled very carefully. The approach at this stage will set the tone for future meetings and discussions. The purpose is to introduce the ideas behind the programme for improving services. Please remember: ■ talk with people and not 'at' them; ■ listen and treat peoples' views as important; ■ be very clear about what the programme is offering and what it is not offering.	Tool 1 Preparing users and community groups for action planning
Preparing users for action planning	Fieldwork teams begin work ■ gain the confidence of local people ■ explore existing attitudes to planning ■ convince people of the need for planning ■ explain how the proposed planning process will work and how long everything may take	Tool 1 Preparing users and community groups for action planning Tool 2 Participatory information gathering Tool 3 The role of NGOs

Table 3a.1. continued

Activity	Brief description	Further guidance
	■ explore the existence of local user groups, other CBOs and active NGOs ■ begin to identify possible roles for local NGOs ■ identify where there is a need to establish new user groups	
Find out what is already there	Initial survey work to find out about what services exist and what are the users perceptions of the services. There are two approaches, both of which need to be used as they provide different information about the same problem. ■ use participatory methods to find out what the opinions of the users are concerning the provision and operation of existing services. This also gives useful indications of demand. ■ also use a technical survey to establish what infrastructure exists, its condition, and where it is located.	Tools 4 Initial survey and groundwork Tool 5 Users perceptions of existing services
Assess users priorities and demand	Use participatory techniques to make an initial assessment of user priorities for improved services: ■ establish what services people want; ■ explore the desire for different levels of service in each sector. Beware of simply asking people what they want without putting any limits on it; otherwise, the natural response is to want everything. The assess-ment needs to revolve around: ■ what do you want? ■ how much of the available development budget are you willing to allocate to this? ■ how much additional contri-bution are you prepared to make to get what you want?	Tool 7 User demand for service improvements also Tool 8 Gender issues Tool 9 Formation of user groups

Table 3a.1. continued

Activity	Brief description	Further guidance
Identify need for promotion activities	■ Depending upon the priorities expressed by users, there may be some important overall goals which the programme wishes to achieve which do not emerge: for example, greater coverage of latrines for improved sanita- tion. ■ In this case it is appropriate to plan for a sanitation promotion programme.	Tool 7 User demand for service improve- ments
Explore technical options and costs	If we are to respond to what people want and are willing to contribute their resources to, we need to be able to offer a range of technical options ■ identify the range of options for providing those services which are a priority ■ narrow down the options to those which are feasible within the local situation; when the specific local site conditions are taken into account, many options do not turn out to be feasible, and this makes the choices more straightforward ■ calculate the indicative costs for the improvements in each sector which the users have prioritised. The use of simple tools such as standard engineering details and spreadsheets makes this relatively simple to do.	Tools 6 Technical options and levels of service
Discuss operation & maintenance requirements	The key issue is that O&M is an essential consideration from the very beginning of the planning process not something which comes in at the end. Users are concerned about how well their services work; this depends on effective O&M of the installed facilities.	See Section 6 on O&M also Tool 6 Technical options and levels of service Tool 9 Formation of user groups

Table 3a.1. continued

Activity	Brief description	Further guidance
	■ new facilities bring with them new requirements for O&M; this is an integral part of deciding which technical option is most suitable. ■ there are different models for the management of O&M, involving the municipality, user groups and individual households to different extents. ■ negotiating roles and responsibilities for O&M is a central part of the consensus building component of action planning.	
Review costs	Discuss the cost estimates with the users in relation to the budget ceiling for the area and willingness to pay for particular levels of service. Users will be contributing to the operation and maintenance costs, and in some cases to the capital costs.	Tool 7 User demand for service improvements Tool 10 Cost recovery
Reassess user priorities and demand	Reviewing the costs may result in changes in demand and user priorities. Assist users to revise their priorities within the overall budget ceiling including any top-up money users/user groups are prepared to add. This now provides the basis for the Local Action Plan.	Tool 7 User demand for service improvements also Tool 8 Gender issues Tool 9 Formation of user groups
Modify technical details	The review of priorities and demand may lead to a desire to modify specific technical details; whilst these can appear to be minor, they may be very important for users: for example, bathing enclosures to suit the specific needs of women.	See Section 5 on Implementation
Engineering design	Detailed engineering design work then needs to be carried out to determine the required capacity and hence the size of water pipes, surface drains, sewers and power	See Section 3b Tool 13 Assessing system capacity

Table 3a.1. continued

Activity	Brief description	Further guidance
	lines. This also needs to specify the how and where this local infrastructure links into the secondary city infrastructure lines.	
Cost recovery	Explore mechanisms for collecting money for both formal payments to municipalities and utilities, and local systems managed by user groups.	Tool 10 Cost recovery
Implementation procedures	Discuss the options for implementing the improvements; in particular, whether there are community based organisations which are interested in undertaking simple works themselves through community contracting.	See Section 5 on Implementation
Draw up Local Action Plan	The Local Action Plan can now be drawn up. It then goes forward to the consensus building process for negotiation and agreement in relation to the Area Service Plan.	See Section 3c on Consensus Building

Cross cutting issues

There are two important issues which need to be considered in each of the steps of the framework in Table 3a.1; these are the 'cross-cutting' issues of gender and user groups.

Gender Issues: women are largely responsible for accessing services such as water for their families. Improvements to services therefore have a particular impact on the time, effort and money which women spend on these activities. Local Action Plans must reflect the fact that:

- women have these responsibilities; and
- women usually know more about the problems of accessing services than men.

Focusing on the priorities of women and children is necessary if the health and social benefits of service improvements are to be realised. For further guidance see:

- Tool 8 Gender issues
- Tool 2 Participatory information gathering

- Tool 3 The role of NGOs

User Groups: Some services are likely to be provided on a communal rather than an individual basis, for example standposts and handpumps for water supply. Maintenance problems are lessened if there are clearly defined groups of users for any service which is not provided to individual households. For further guidance see:

- Tool 9 Formation of user groups

Preparing the Local Action Plan

The important point here is that the Local Action Plan as described in the Framework (Table 3a.1) is something which develops from a set of initial proposals, followed by discussions and revisions of these proposals. There is always an important element of negotiation, 'going round and round' to arrive at an eventual solution which is the best compromise between the possible options and the available resources.

The final stage is to present all of the ideas which have been developed; this is an essential record of who has agreed to do what. It is very important to realise that the ideas contained in the plan may need to be expressed in different ways for the different stakeholder groups.

- People from urban poor communities may not be familiar with formally written-up plans, calculations and drawings; verbal communication and verbal agreements/contracts are commonplace. It is important to have a record of what has been agreed; this can be contained on a site plan which has been developed using participatory techniques. Nevertheless, some users are quite comfortable with more formally presented plans.
- Secondary stakeholders including donor/lending agencies require plans to be drawn up and submitted using formats which are specific to the agency; try to find out what formats and procedures are required and use these. Sometimes this can create problems for local Programme Managers, because external agencies do not always make it clear what they require.

It is important to develop a simple, consistent reporting format. The fieldwork teams have primary responsibility for preparing the plan in the agreed format and to make sure that the contents are signed off by representatives of the users, possibly through CBOs and/or NGOs.

Table 3a.2. suggests what information the Local Action Plan should contain.

Table 3a.2. Typical contents of the Local Action Plan

Section	Contents
1. Existing situation	■ location of existing services marked on a site plan ■ summary of users perceptions of the adequacy of existing services
2. User priorities	■ summary of the agreed priorities
3. Proposal for improvement	■ list proposed service improvements by sector (see Table 3a.3 below) ■ identify specific user groups with 'communal' facilities such as water points, shared latrines and solid waste bins ■ mark up the site plan with location of new facilities and service lines ■ cross reference each service improvement to Standard Engineering Details (see Section 5 From Action Plans to Implementation); specify any modifications to these standard details
4. Design Calculations	■ detailed engineering designs and specifications for water pipelines, surface drains, sewers, power lines. Use standard details wherever possible. This section can be placed in an Appendix. ■ relevant details such as pipe size can be included on the site plan
5. Cost estimates	■ prepare a table of indicative cost estimates for the improvements by sector
6. Proposal for financing	■ set out how the improvements will be financed ■ list the financial commitments and contributions to be made by agencies and users against the different facilities
7. Operation and Maintenance	■ list O&M tasks by sector for each of the improvements ■ define roles and responsibilities for tasks with a list of commitments made by agencies and users
8. Cost recovery	■ define the mechanisms for paying for user contributions to capital costs ■ specify how O&M costs are to be collected and paid to the different agencies; this is particularly important for shared facilities
9. Implementation	■ proposals for implementation to list which agency will be responsible for the different improvements ■ proposed works to be undertaken by community contract

Table 3a.3 gives examples of proposals which might arise during the planning process and would need to be detailed as part of section 3 in the suggested Action Plan structure of Table 3a.2 above. Note that not all of these will necessarily arise as part of the Action Plan.

Table 3a.3. Examples of required inputs to Local Action Plans	
Sector	**Proposal for improvement**
Water Supply	■ number and location of individual connections ■ number and location of communal supply points ■ location and type of aprons and bathing enclosures ■ identification of specific user groups ■ location of existing and proposed water supply lines
Sanitation/ sewerage	■ number and location of individual household latrines ■ number and location of shared latrines ■ identification of specific user groups ■ location of existing and proposed sewer lines (for sewered sanitation only)
Drainage	■ location and type of existing and new drains
Flood protection	■ location and height of retaining walls
Access and Paving	■ location and type of paving ■ location and details of any revisions to access widths
Security lighting	■ number, type and location of security lights ■ location of power lines and ancillary equipment (transformers etc.)
Power supply	■ location of individual connections
Solid waste management	■ individual household collection ■ communal user group collection ■ identification of specific user groups
Community Buildings	■ location ■ plinth area ■ materials of construction

Tools to support local action planning

The following tools have been developed to support the activities required to carry out local action planning; you will find these in the following part of this section of the manual. The Framework for action planning (Table 3a.1) also makes reference to tools in other sections of the manual.

Table 3a.4. Supporting tools for local action planning	
Tool	**Description**
1.	Preparing users and community groups for action planning
2.	Participatory information gathering
3.	The role of NGOs
4.	Initial survey and groundwork
5.	User perceptions of existing services
6.	Technical options and levels of service
7.	User demand for service improvements
8.	Gender issues
9.	Formation of user groups
10.	Cost recovery

Tool 1 Preparing users and community groups for action planning

How this tool will help you

This tool will help you with the activities:

- establishing contact; and
- preparing users for action planning listed in Table 3a.1.

Using this tool

It provides guidance on how you can:

- introduce local residents and community groups to the benefits of action planning; and
- prepare them to take an active part in that process.

Structure of the tool

The tool is structured around the following questions:

- Why involve users and community groups in action planning?
- Why is preparation for action planning required?
- Who should prepare people for action planning?
- When and where should preparation for action planning start?
- What are the stages in preparing people for action planning and what does each stage require?

Each question is now considered in turn.

Why involve users and community groups in action planning?

Service users and the community groups that represent them should be involved in action planning for the following reasons.

- **To ensure that the proposals contained in Action Plans meet their requirements**. If local people are not involved in the process, there is no guarantee that the action taken will meet their actual and perceived needs.

- **To provide access to local knowledge** Local people know things about their area that may not be obvious to outsiders. Some of this knowledge will be about social structures and relationships but they are also likely to know a lot about the location and performance of existing services.

- **To ensure that local power-brokers are involved in the planning process**. All too often, plans produced by professionals fail because they do not take into account the concerns and likely actions of local power brokers such as ward councillors and ward committee members.

- **To develop an integrated approach to the allocation of resources** Communities are not homogenous entities and different groups are likely to have different concerns and priorities. Action Plans provide an opportunity to mediate between the demands of different groups and arrive at an agreed approach to the utilisation of scarce resources.

Why is preparation for action planning required?

Preparation of service users and community groups for action planning will normally be required for two reasons.

- **To convince them of the need for action planning.** People living in low-income areas have a whole range of pressing concerns and will be reluctant to give up their time for an exercise for which they see no clear use. In particular, they may question the need for planning, saying that they already know their needs and how to achieve them.

- **To provide them with the skills required to plan effectively**. Everyone plans in one way or another but most people plan individually without ever setting things down in a formal way. Few participants in the planning exercise will have experience of formal planning, involving the need to agree shared objectives and then to prioritise those objectives. Users and the community groups that represent them will not be effective participants in the planning process unless some effort is given to provide them with these skills.

Who should prepare people for action planning?

A fieldwork team is required to prepare people to take part in action planning. It should include people who have experience of working with the communities with which you wish to engage. They may come from government departments such as community development cells and also involve NGOs that are already working with communities. See Table 3.a.1.

As you identify the members of the fieldwork team, you will need to provide them with training so that they are aware of the main features of the action planning approach. Ideally, the training should cover:

- the action planning processes to be used;

- an introduction to participatory methods, with particular emphasis on methods for ensuring that the poor and marginalised are included in the action planning process. See Tool 2 for further details.

- negotiation and conflict resolution; and

- an introduction to the way in which government systems work and the probable availability of resources.

When and where should preparation for action planning start?

As soon as a decision to adopt an action planning process has been made, you need to think about preparing users and community groups to take part in that process. It may be that you decide to carry out some pilot work to develop the planning process at the local level. Where this is the case, the initial focus should be on preparing the people living in potential pilot areas to take part in the process.

What are the stages in preparing people for action planning and what does each stage require?

The following actions may be required to prepare potential service users and the community groups that represent them for action planning.

1. Gain the confidence of potential participants.

2. Explore existing attitudes to planning.

3. Convince people of the value of planning if exploration of existing attitudes shows that this is needed.

4. Ensure that people understand the proposed planning process.

Gain the confidence of potential participants. Action planning cannot succeed if the intended participants have no confidence in the process. People may well be suspicious of government because of the latter's lack of interest or failure to deliver in the past. The best way to gain people's confidence is to talk with them in a way that convinces them that you respect them and want to hear about how they perceive their problems and possible solutions to those problems. One way of doing this is to involve groups of local people in participatory mapping. See Box T1.1.

Box T1.1. Participatory mapping

Participatory mapping is a simple process through which groups of community members are encouraged to draw maps of their own communities, indicating what they think is important. They will normally indicate all the houses or compounds, together with important facilities and physical features. Most texts on participatory mapping suggest that the maps should be drawn on the ground using locally available materials. However, experience suggests that a more conventional approach using paper and markers will normally be more appropriate in urban areas.
As the map is developed, encourage the group to indicate any social groupings within their area as this may later provide a basis for choosing representatives for the planning process. It can also provide information on particular marginalised groups, which might not always be obvious to outsiders.

Explore existing attitudes to planning. Exploring people's existing attitudes to planning will help to determine what needs to be done to ensure that they are willing to contribute to the action planning process. Use **interviews with key informants** and **focus group discussions** to explore these attitudes. Key informants might include political representatives, community 'leaders', representatives of community organisations, and local people with particular skills and knowledge. Ideally, these key informants should include those who have previously been involved in efforts to provide or obtain improved infrastructures services. When searching out local people with skills and knowledge, look particularly for those who have been involved in either construction initiatives or in activities such as health promotion, basic education and encouraging and facilitating community-based activities.

Focus groups should represent particular interest groups within the community. They might include people from particular social groups or those with particular occupations. Remember to hold focus group discussions with different age groups and with both women and men.

In addition to exploring attitudes to planning, interviews with key informants provide an opportunity to identify those who might take a leading role in the process. Ask people which people in their community have been most active in trying to improve their own situation and that of the neighbourhood. Such 'activists' are likely to be among the most receptive to the idea of action planning.

Convince people of the need for planning. It is probable that the initial investigation of people's attitudes will show that they see little need for formal planning. Where this is the case, they must be convinced of the need for planning before you can proceed to the implementation of an action planning process. How might this be done? You might:

1. Develop awareness of the problems that might arise because of failure to plan.

2. Show people the benefits that planning can bring.

Start to do the first by encouraging people to discuss the way in which decisions are made at present. Ask them to list the initiatives that they and various government agencies have taken in the area. To help them to remember what has been done, encourage people to look around the area and remind themselves of what has been done. Next ask people to consider what was good and what was bad about those initiatives. In particular, encourage them to consider the problems that might have arisen because of a lack of planning. Ask them whether the initiatives taken by government were really what they wanted and whether they have other priorities that have not been considered by government.

By the end of this process, people should have started to think about the weaknesses of ad-hoc unplanned approaches to service provision. You can then perhaps ask them to consider how things might have been different if there had been an Action Plan *to which they had contributed.*

Where suitable examples exist, it may be possible to arrange a visit to an area where people have been involved in an action planning process. Assuming that the action planning process has been successful, this will provide them with clear evidence of the advantages of planning. Try to ensure that there are good opportunities for the people from the two communities to talk with each other. People are more likely to be convinced by what is said by people like themselves than by ideas presented by external professionals who may speak and think in a way that is not familiar to them.

Box T1.2. Who should be targeted?

While the ideal is that all community members should be convinced of the need for an action planning process, the reality is that some people will become more involved in the process than others. It is best if you concentrate your efforts on these people, who will then provide a lead for other people. They may include recognised community leaders but equally they may be people who see a role for themselves in the action planning process and are willing to work hard to fulfil that role. Where your initial investigations have shown that there are distinct social groups within the community, you should try to ensure that all social groups are represented. Do not forget that women make up about 50% of the population and that their priorities are likely to be different from those of men. Their concerns will only be addressed if they are given a prominent role in the planning process.

Explain the process. Once there is at least a basic acceptance of the need for planning, the next step is to explain the process to people. This will be easier if the planning process is built around existing structures and systems. This might mean, for instance that the planning process is based on existing groupings wherever possible. An example from Sri Lanka is provided in Box T1.3.

Box T1.3. Working through existing organisations and organisational structures

In 1984, the Government of Sri Lanka launched its Million Houses Programme (MHP), a programme designed to bring about improvements in housing at an affordable price. The Urban Housing Division of the National Housing Development Authority (NHDA) was formed to deal with urban housing needs in 1985. One important aspect of its pro-gramme was a participatory planning approach that brought together community members in low income areas, officials of the NHDA and employees of the local author-ity in order to develop a 'micro plan' for each low-income settlement.

The vehicles for project implementation at the local level were community development councils (CDCs). The CDC concept had already been developed in the course of a previous UNICEF project that focused mainly on health. The NHDA project designers decided to use the CDCs rather than develop new organisations specifically for the micro-planning work. This did not mean that every settlement already had a CDC but existing CDCs were used where they existed and new CDCs were set up where neces-sary. This is a good example of working from what already exists rather than setting up a completely new structure.

When explaining the process, remember the following simple rules:

- keep it simple;
- be clear about what people will be expected to do; and
- be clear about the intended outcome.

Base your explanation on the processes set out in sections 3a, 3b and 3c of this manual.

For local plans involving a small area and relatively few people, it may be possible to speak to everyone who may be affected by the plan. For larger areas a better approach will be to identify people who can take the message to other people in the community. You might for instance identify a person from each area to be included in the planning process and involve them in a workshop to explain the process to be followed. They can then carry out a similar exercise with people living in their own areas.

Tool 2 Participatory information gathering

How this tool will help you

This tool will provide you with an overview of participatory information gathering in relation to urban services provision for urban poor groups. It does not go into the detailed application of the various techniques described, but refers you on to other sources of information. It also provides a number of examples based on a study of Operations and Maintenance performance in an Indian city. It will help you with the activities

- team building; and
- preparing users for action planning

in the Framework for local action planning (Table 3a.1).

Using this tool

There exists a wide range of participatory tools and techniques; use Table T2.1 to compare the advantages and disadvantages of these. Refer to the examples to see the value and richness of the information which can emerge. Read this in conjunction with Tool 1 on preparing community groups for action planning.

Users can tell you about the service

In any performance measurement system for services such as water supply and sanitation provision, it is essential is to obtain the views of the users of the service. Whilst the importance of consumer perceptions is clearly understood by the commercial and industrial sectors of the economy, user perceptions about water and sanitation services are frequently neglected.

So how do the users perceive the operating performance of the service? An important feature of this is the need to be *inclusive*; that is, to include the views of the urban poor as well as those in middle and high income areas of cities. This means that reviewing customer complaints is unlikely to be sufficient, and we need to look more deeply into using participative techniques to elicit the views of the poor who rarely have access to the formal channels through which complaints are made.

Participatory approaches

The methodologies used for collecting information clearly depend upon the local setting. It may be that participation is being developed through other programmes, and it is thereby possible to pick up on service related issues relatively easily as community groups will already have been exposed to participatory information gathering.

There is a place for both quantitative and qualitative data. Quantitative methods expose 'what' and 'how much', whereas qualitative methods have explanatory value and answer the question 'why'. This is one of the great strengths of participatory methods. Finding out whether something is working or not may be insufficient to plan effective remedial actions; we need to know and understand *why* there are problems to make sure that the root causes can be addressed, rather than just the symptoms.

Table T2.1 reviews some techniques which employ varying degrees of participation.

Table T2.1. Some participatory methods

Method	Advantages	Disadvantages	Alternatives/Keep in mind
Public meetings	■ The audience will contain many different interests, with different levels of understanding and sympathy	■ It is difficult to keep to a fixed agenda ■ Only a few people get a chance to have a say	■ Identify and meet key interests informally ■ Run workshop sessions for different interest groups ■ Bring people together after the workshop sessions in a report-back seminar
Formal survey	■ Questionnaires, studies and in-depth discussion groups can be a good way to start the participation process	■ Surveys are insufficient on their own	■ Surveys require expert design and piloting ■ Surveyors need training ■ Survey design can be part of a process which leads to action
Consultative committee	■ Some focus for decision-making will be necessary in anything beyond a simple consultation process	■ Even if a committee is elected or drawn from key interest groups it may not be a channel for reaching most people ■ People invited to join a committee may feel uncomfortable about being seen as representatives	■ The committee can help to plan the participation process ■ Surveys, workshops and informal meetings to identify other people who may become actively involved ■ A range of groups working on different issues
Working through NGOs/CBOs	■ Voluntary bodies such as NGOs/CBOs are a major route to communities of interest and may have people and resources to contribute to the participation process ■ They have a wealth of experience and are essential allies	■ Voluntary bodies however are not 'the community'	■ There will be many small community groups who are not part of the more formalised voluntary sector ■ Voluntary groups have their own agendas; they are not neutral
Participatory Rapid Appraisal (PRA)	■ If done well, the work belongs to the local people	■ Care needs to be exercised in choosing appropriate tools	■ A range of tools are available (see the following section)

Participatory Rapid Appraisal (PRA)

Time and resource constraints often do not permit extensive social research to be carried out. Instead, the techniques of participatory rapid appraisal (PRA) can be used. An important feature of using participatory methods is that local people are directly involved in the processes of data gathering and analysis. The findings belong to them rather than to the outsiders (always assuming that the PRA work is well done). This gives a wider context to PRA, in that it contributes to a shared learning agenda and local capacity building as well as to the process of information exchange. The following summary of PRA sources and activities is taken from Section 2.2 of the DFID *Guidance Manual on Water and Sanitation Programmes* (WELL, 1998).

Some PRA Techniques

- Secondary data sources, maps and reports
- Direct observation
- Case studies, work, and incident histories from local experts
- Transect walks: systematically walking through an area with local guides, observing, asking, listening and learning about relevant issues
- Group discussions of different kinds (casual, focus, community)
- Mapping and modelling to show local world views
- Matrix scoring and ranking exercises to compare preferences and conditions
- Well-being grouping to establish local criteria for deprivation and disadvantage
- Time-lines and trend and change analysis to show chronologies of events and to analyse local trends and causes of change
- Seasonal calendars and daily time use analysis to show work patterns and activities

For more details on these and other tools see Narayan (1993).

Using participatory approaches

Participatory approaches are used to find out about users perceptions of services and their demand for improvements. It is important to appreciate that the whole process is quite different from the strict question-and-answer method which characterises the objective external evaluation methods. Therefore in using participatory approaches, it is important to define key objectives and to keep these in mind when briefing the facilitators of, for example, the PRA approach. Section 6 of the Manual includes some examples of the use of PRA with respect to Operation and Maintenance.

A further benefit of using participatory approaches is that we find out a lot of relevant background information about the community in question. This can be crucially important to planning remedial measures and subsequent improvements. Such findings are often qualitative in nature; nevertheless, such information is very important in building up a picture of the perception of services in a low income community.

Whilst the more general picture is invaluable, it is important to ensure that PRA finds out from the users where the main problems lie, and looks at options for overcoming them.

Do's and don'ts

The following list indicates some of the key points which should be taken into consideration in the collection of information using participatory methods.

DO	DON'T	ABOVE ALL
■ Find out about taboos and norms	■ Violate taboos and norms	■ Listen and be interested
■ Stimulate people to talk	■ Demand appreciation	■ Respect the people, their perceptions and their knowledge
■ Provide facts and information	■ Use abstract language	
■ Build up a dialogue	■ Interrupt, blame, suggest or promise	
■ Be neutral and objective	■ Side with opinion leaders or agitate	
■ Assist people to evaluate	■ Manipulate or create needs	
■ Be patient		
■ Be creative, adaptable and innovative		
■ Learn from 'errors'		
■ Use analogy		
■ Use a variety of PRA techniques		
■ Cross-check information		

References

Narayan, D. P., (1993) *Participatory Evaluation: Tools for managing change in water and sanitation,* World Bank Technical Paper No. 207, World Bank, Washington DC

WELL, (1998) *Guidance Manual on Water Supply and Sanitation Programmes*

Tool 3 The role of NGOs

How this tool will help you

This tool will help you to understand the ways in which NGOs can be involved in upgrading programmes. It will do this by describing the ways in which NGOs work with local communities, keeping in mind their potential strengths and weaknesses.

Using this tool

Read the first part of the tool if you require information on the starting points for NGO involvement in service provision. Refer to Table T3.1 for a summary of the tasks that might be undertaken by NGOs and the way in which the starting point affects likely NGO roles. The final part provides further information on NGO roles in these various tasks.

Possible starting points for NGO involvement in service provision

NGOs as a catalyst for people's own efforts. Most low-income areas suffer from service deficiencies, because government has either not provided basic services or failed to maintain those that are provided. In such circumstances, community members sometimes combine to provide and manage a shared facility, for instance a well or a local sewer. There are two problems with such unaided attempts to provide services:

- the design and construction are often technically unsound; and
- lack of co-ordination means that actions are often small-scale and ad-hoc.

NGOs can provide assistance to overcome these problems by:

- providing technical advice and assistance;
- encouraging people to see problems in their overall context; and
- helping them to organise themselves so as to tackle their problems in a co-ordinated way.

In effect, the role of the NGO is to act as a catalyst, persuading people to work together and, where appropriate, guiding their efforts. NGOs that have acted in this way include the Orangi Pilot Project (OPP) in Pakistan, SPARC in India and Sevanatha in Sri Lanka. The important point to note is that this type of action is always started either by the NGO itself or by local community leaders working in association with the NGO.

NGOs as facilitators of government projects and programmes. In recent years, there has been increased emphasis on the need for community involvement in 'official' upgrading programmes. Since few service providing departments and agencies have experience of working with communities, some other way of linking government with communities must be found. Specialist community development cells within municipalities or a social welfare ministry may be used for this purpose where they exist. However, it is also common to assume that NGOs can and should fulfil this role.

This manual is concerned primarily with government-initiated programmes and so the main focus will be on the role of NGOs as facilitators. It is commonly assumed that this role requires that NGOs are contracted to government departments. Another model, in which NGOs operate as partners and act as catalysts as well as facilitators is described in Box T3.1.

Box T3.1. NGOs as partners in government programmes

It is possible to develop an upgrading programme on the basis that any proposal can be considered for inclusion in the programme provided that it meets the programme's basic requirements. These requirements will normally be that the proposal is presented by a group representing the community and conforms with standard programme guidelines in such areas as the arrangements for cost-sharing, the involvement of disadvantaged community members and perhaps the development of an action plan to guide investment.

NGOs would be essential to the success of this approach, working with communities to help them to determine their needs and develop proposals for funding. In effect, NGOs would be working as project partners. This model goes beyond the 'NGO as facilitator' model in two respects.

- The focus of the NGO and the community groups that it is supporting may go beyond the sectors covered by the project or programme so that they see the latter as one among several possible sources of funding and support.
- The role of the NGO is to bring communities into the project or programme rather than working with a pre-selected community.

This is a conceptually attractive approach in that it ensures that a project really responds to demand. It has two potential drawbacks. The first of these is the possible difficulty in ensuring the involvement of the poorest communities in the project or programme. Training and orientation to sensitise NGO staff to the need to engage with the poorest

---

Box T3.1. (continued)

communities will help to overcome this problem. The second problem is that NGOs may not be willing to 'compromise' their principles sufficiently to allow them to work in the way required by a government programme. This is a potentially difficult problem. The best way to overcome it will be to ensure that potential NGO partners are fully involved in the project design.

Note that a mechanism will have to be found to cover the costs of 'partnering' NGOs. One approach might be to pay them a 'management fee' for the projects that they facilitate. Another might be to register NGOs as partners and pay them an agreed yearly amount.

How does the starting point affect the role of NGOs?

The starting point for NGO involvement in service provision is likely to affect the tasks that the NGO is called upon to perform and may affect the way in which it approaches them. Table T3.1 provides further information in relation to this point.

Table T3.1. Likely effect of starting point on the tasks to be undertaken by NGOs

Task	NGO as facilitator of government/community interaction	NGO as catalyst for community action
Develop community awareness of problems	Main focus on problems that the government project or programme is designed to solve.	All problems can be considered in first instance.
Develop community awareness of possibilities	Focus on how communities can engage with government project to solve problems.	Focus on what community can do to either solve problems itself or persuade others to help to solve them.
Assist people to organise themselves	NGOs will normally work within parameters set by project.	Different NGOs may take different approaches.
Facilitate action planning process	NGO personnel may take leading role. Government may engage external NGO as workshop organiser/ facilitator.	NGO personnel may take leading role in promoting and organising action planning process.

Table T3.1. continued

Task	NGO as facilitator of government/ community interaction	NGO as catalyst for community action
Provide support during design and implementation	NGO may facilitate links between technical staff and communities.	NGO may develop systems and provide technical support.
Develop monitoring and evaluation systems	An external NGO with relevant skills may be engaged to develop aspects of a project/ programme monitoring and evaluation system.	NGO may develop information system.
Carry out impact assessment	An external NGO is sometimes engaged to carry out an impact assessment.	May be done informally but rarely formally.

The remainder of this tool considers the roles of NGOs in relation to the various tasks listed in Table T3.1.

Develop community awareness of problems

The important point here is to be aware of what NGOs are to be expected to do. If their role is to facilitate links between government and communities for a specific project or programme, they must focus on the sectors that the project will cover. If an NGO is working as a catalyst for community development and action, it will probably have a rather wider remit. However, it must be able to identify the problems that the project or programme is designed to tackle and ensure that the community is aware of those problems and of the possibilities for tackling them presented by the project or programme.

Sometimes NGOs have experience of participatory techniques but have limited understanding of how these techniques can be used in pursuit of the target of improved service provision. In such cases, NGO personnel will probably need to be given training and guidance on how participatory appraisal methods can be used in a problem-orientated way.

Some basic rules for awareness-raising are presented in Box T3.2.

Box T3.2. Two basic rules for awareness-raising

1. Keep working methods as simple as possible. For instance, use slides showing the adverse impacts of poor sanitation and drainage on the local environment to develop community awareness and promote discussion on the need for improved services.

2. Whenever possible, use methods that help people to identify problems themselves. For instance, encourage community members to make their own videos and record interviews on problems caused by service deficiencies. Where some NGOs have experience of using such methods, it may be appropriate to arrange workshops at which they can share their expertise with other, less experienced NGOs.

Develop community awareness of possibilities

Some NGOs will have technical expertise that enables them to help communities to identify the possibilities for service improvement in any given situation. However, many NGOs are more comfortable with the human than the technical aspects of development. Beware of NGOs with a strong commitment to one technology since they are likely to assume that this technology should be used in all circumstances.

Where an NGO has social expertise but little technical knowledge, there are two options.

1. To provide training to the NGO's personnel to provide them with the knowledge required to guide communities on the possibilities open to them.

2. To arrange for the NGO to work in association with another organisation that has the requisite technical knowledge. This organisation might be a government department, a consulting company or another NGO.

The second option will often be the better one, provided that the two organisations can agree on the approach to be followed. A good approach will be for the NGO to work with community members to identify problems and needs, after which the technical organisation presents the available technical options and some guidance on their limitations, advantages and disadvantages. The NGO might then act as facilitator in the dialogue between community members and technical specialists on the choice of technology and approach.

Assisting people to organise themselves

Because they are people-centred and reasonably flexible, NGOs are often better placed than government organisations to help communities to organise themselves for action planning. This is particularly true if they are already known and trusted in the community. However, not all NGOs have equal commitment and expertise. When considering the use of NGOs to help people to organise, you should ask the following questions:

- Do existing NGOs with the required approach and skills exist? If not, how might they be provided with the required training and orientation? It may be that NGOs with good experience of community organisation can be used to provide guidance to less experienced local NGOs.

- Is there clarity about **why** people should organise?

- Is there clarity about **how** people should organise?

The best way to tackle the last two questions will be for all stakeholders, including NGOs, to agree on the approach to be taken **before** extensive work starts in the field.

Facilitating action planning

Their people-centred approach can make NGOs a good choice for facilitating action planning. Indeed, the identification of problems and possible solutions, the development of community organisational structures and action planning should be viewed together rather than separately. NGO personnel that have worked with local communities should certainly be involved in the action planning process.

Specialist skills are required to facilitate workshops. It may be best if people from NGOs other than those who have been working closely with communities facilitate action planning workshops. NGOs with experience of participatory approaches are among the most likely to possess the specialist skills required for this task.

Support during design and implementation

NGOs may provide inputs at the design and implementation stages in two ways.

1. By providing technical inputs.

2. By providing a link between technical personnel and the community.

NGOs that act as catalysts for community effort are more likely to fulfil the first role. In many cases, these NGOs will have a more positive view of appropriate standards and methods of working than government engineers. Nevertheless, you should ensure that NGOs do not attempt to take on tasks that fall beyond their technical competence. If in doubt, work with the NGO and other stakeholders to reach agreement on the overall technical approach, design details and design standards. Where necessary, test aspects of the approach to be used so that you have hard information upon which choices can be made.

Designers need to liaise with communities on decisions such as the service level to be provided and the siting of communal facilities. NGOs that are working closely with the community may be in a good position to facilitate this liaison. Later, trouble-free implementation of schemes is much more likely if local residents have access to channels through which they can express their concerns to government departments and their contractors. NGOs should not normally be involved directly in this liaison but they may be consulted on how effective channels of communication may be established.

Monitoring and evaluation/impact assessment
It may be appropriate to involve NGOs with suitable experience in the development of monitoring and evaluation systems and the collection of information for such systems. NGOs may also be called upon to carry out impact assessments. When considering such roles for NGOs, think about the task in hand and the knowledge and skills required to undertake it. In general, only those NGOs with considerable specialist knowledge of information systems and impact assessment are likely to have the resources to develop systems. Similarly, participatory evaluation and impact assessment require special skills and only NGOs with appropriate resources should be considered for these tasks. In such cases, the role of the NGO will be essentially that of a contractor.

Tool 4 Initial survey and groundwork

How this tool will help you

This tool will help you to carry out the activity *Find out what is already there* in the Framework for local action planning (see Section 3a, Table 3a.1). The tool contains a series of checklists which you can use to help you in the technical surveys which need to be carried out to establish what infrastructure exists and where it is located. Note that this only provides part of the answer; we need the information obtained by finding out about users perceptions of the existing services as outlined in Tool 5 to complete the picture.

Using this tool

Use the following checklists for each service sector to identify services in the neighbourhood; remember to make full use of any available maps and plans which you have obtained from the municipality and utilities (see Section 3b Table 3b.1, Framework for action planning for networked services). This work is objective in nature and needs to involve an engineer and a surveyor. However, note that it is essential that the survey team ask local residents what they know about the location of service lines.

You should also look at Section 3b, Tool 13 *Assessing system capacity*; this is aimed at the secondary and primary networked infrastructure, but it has important implications for the local neighbourhood (tertiary) services.

General points

It is important to establish basic information such as:

- initial definition of boundaries of the upgrading areas;
- estimated number of households and population;
- land tenure status; and
- socio-economic status of residents.

These issues are best addressed using participatory methods rather than as part of the 'checklist' surveys described in this Tool; see Tools 1,2 and 3.

Access and Paving

Date of survey

Survey Team

Name of site

Location

Sketch plan of the site indicating:

- road and access way widths;
- distinguish between through routes and access-only streets;
- any encroachments or aspects which hinder access;
- paved widths (when less than the total right of way); and
- service lines (water, drainage, sewerage, power) which restrict access.

Describe the type and condition of existing surfacing

Describe any drainage problems which occur as a result of inadequate surfacing

Predominant type of traffic on the various roads

Location of institutions, commercial and industrial premises which generate high traffic volumes and loadings

Any further comments

Water supply

Date of survey

Survey Team

Name of site

Location

Sources of water: piped supply; tubewell; open well; rainwater; others

Number and location of drinking water and bathing water supply points: public standposts, house taps, others (indicate on site plan)

Reliability of water supply; supply times (daily and seasonal)

Approximate pressure of water supplied (piped supply only)

Visual quality, taste and odour of water from each source

Size and adequacy of local secondary distribution mains

Sewage disposal system: leaching pit; septic tank; sewer; open drain; other

Any further comments

Drainage

Date of survey

Survey Team

Name of site

Location

On your site map indicate:

- existing surface water drains, showing dimensions;
- drainage outfall points;
- secondary drains, showing dimensions; and
- low-lying areas (depressions) which give problems.

Sullage disposal for households and public water supply points

Physical condition of site drains and outfalls

Physical condition of secondary drains

Frequency and causes of flooding

Road surfacing and paving

Any further comments

Solid waste management

Date of survey

Survey Team

Name of site

Location

Evidence and extent of problems: waste in drains; roadside and indiscriminate dumping (mark on map)

Location and condition of communal containers and transfer station (if existing)

Approximate generation rates from households, shops, commercial and small industry premises

Apparent composition of waste

Collection frequency from collection points

What is the involvement of municipal and private sweepers

How regularly are streets swept

Do people have bins or containers inside houses

Do households sell recyclable components of waste

Any further comments

Power supply and street lighting

Date of survey

Survey Team

Name of site

Location

On your map of the site indicate:

- overhead or underground power cables;
- transformers; and
- street lights.

Approximate number of household power connections with meters

What electrical appliances are most commonly used in the home

Evidence of illegal power connections

Type of street light: lamp source (fluorescent, mercury vapour, high or low pressure sodium, other)

Mounting details of street lights (wall or pole mounted)

On-off switching times and switching mechanism

Approximate number of faulty street lights

Any further comments

Sanitation

Date of survey

Survey Team

Name of site

Location

Anal cleansing practices

Latrine types: household, on-plot, shared, communal, none: if none, locate the defecation areas

General condition of latrines

Excreta disposal system: on/off plot leach pit or septic tank; sewer, open drain, bucket, other

Awareness of importance of sanitation and hygiene

Sources of water for drinking and bathing

Users comments on the effectiveness of their sanitation and how it could be improved

Any further comments

Tool 5 User perceptions of existing services

How this tool will help you

This tool will help you to carry out the activity *Find out what is already there* in the Framework for local action planning (see Section 3a, Table 3a.1). The tool contains a checklist of activities which will help you to find out about users perceptions of the existing services in their neighbourhood and in their homes. This in turn gives useful indications of what the demand for improved services is likely to be and is a way of starting off the whole process of discussing demand with the users. These activities need to be carried out in a participatory way, using some of the participatory techniques described in Tool 2. You need to use the information which you find out here together with that obtained from the initial physical survey described in Tool 4.

Using this tool

Use the Activity Checklist in Table T5.1 to investigate users perceptions for all of the existing services including:

- water supply;
- sanitation;
- drainage;
- flood protection;
- access and paving;
- power and security lighting;
- solid waste management; and
- community buildings.

In addition to finding out what people think, you will also uncover important information relating to roles and responsibilities, that is, who does what. Note that activities and users concerns with any other service issues not included above should also be explored.

Table T5.1. Users perceptions

Activity checklist	Findings
What facilities and services do residents perceive to be lacking?	
What are the actual problems with the day to day operation and maintenance of existing facilities and services?	
Whose responsibility are these problems perceived to be?	
How have problems with the provision of facilities and services been resolved, with particular reference to internal local initiatives?	
Identify actions related to service provision carried out by residents; identify whether residents undertake work themselves or contract a third party	
What are the attitudes and perceptions amongst the users concerning roles and responsibilities for O&M?	

Table T5.1. (continued)

Activity checklist	Findings
Identify actions related to service provision carried out by statutory bodies such as the municipality	
Is there evidence of facilities being cared for by users?	
Is there evidence of facilities being misused?	
Are there any clearly defined user groups, for example, for certain sources of water including water supply points, latrines?	
Are there any mechanisms through which users can approach city institutions; if so what are they and how effectively do they work ?	
What is the potential for promoting increased ownership and care of facilities through users becoming more proactive?	

Table T5.1. (continued)	
Activity checklist	**Findings**
What are the possible routes and mechanisms which could help users to become more proactive?	
Are there any clearly defined user groups for example, for certain sources of water including water supply points, latrines?	
Are there any mechanisms through which users can approach city institutions; if so what are they and how effectively do they work?	
What is the potential for promoting increased ownership and care of facilities through users becoming more proactive?	
What are the possible routes and mechanisms which could help users to become more proactive?	

Tool 6 Technical options and levels of service

How this tool will help you
This tool will help you to carry out the activities *Explore technical options and costs* in the Framework for local action planning (see Table 3a.1. Section 3a). The tool provides a listing of the most common technical options for improving services and includes some basic maintenance tasks which are theoretically within the capability of most user groups. For more detailed guidance on operations and maintenance please refer to Section 6 of this manual. This tool also gives additional guidance on factors which affect levels of service and on estimating indicative costs.

Using this tool
Use the listing of technical options by service sector in Table T6.1 and the factors affecting levels of service in Table T6.2 to guide the discussion during meetings with service users to assist in the following:

- determining which options are technically feasible in the locality (for example if there is no groundwater, handpumps are not an option);

- drawing up a short list of possible options and levels of service which users are interested in and which will form the basis for more detailed exploration of specific designs and costs.

Use Table T6.2 to assist in discussions with the users about different levels of service; the subsequent guidance assists in estimating indicative costs for the preferred options.

Technical options for different services
Table T6.1 lists a wide range of possible technical options. Whilst in theory there is a wide range of infrastructure options from which the users can choose, in practice the choice is limited by both the existing infrastructure and the physical characteristics of the site. This will rapidly become apparent during the discussions you hold.

Further details of technical options are given in *Services for Shelter* by Andrew Cotton and Richard Franceys.

Table T6.1. Service options and maintenance requirements

Water:

OPTION	MAINTENANCE
Standpost	Tap replacement; report leaks
Handpump	Minor repairs; report major faults
Washing aprons	Cleaning
Bathing enclosures:	
Bamboo screens	Replace every two years; cleaning
5" brick walls	Cleaning
Informal rainwater collection	Cleaning of collection containers

Sanitation:

OPTION	MAINTENANCE
Latrines	
Individual household latrine	Daily cleaning
User group shared latrine	Daily cleaning
Disposal system	
On-site pit	Pit emptying
Septic tank	Tank emptying
Sewerage	Report defects

Drainage:

OPTION	MAINTENANCE
Earth fill low lying areas	Occasional replenishment
Road-as-drain	Regular sweeping in front of house
Roadside drain	Regular cleaning in front of house

Pond improvement:

OPTION	MAINTENANCE
Laterite walling	Occasional repair
Paved surround	Regular sweeping
Beautification	Care of plants and trees

Table T6.1. (continued)

Paving:

OPTION	MAINTENANCE
Gravel fill	Occasional replenishment
Brick on edge	Replace broken bricks
Unsealed road metal	Hole patching
Surface dressing	Report defects
Bituminous carpet	Report defects
Cement concrete (CC)	Report defects
Laterite block paving	Replace broken or missing slabs
Precast stepping stones	Replace broken or missing slabs

Security Lighting:

OPTION	MAINTENANCE
RCC poles, 3-line non-insulated cable	Report defects
Wall-mounted single insulated cable	Report defects
Lantern fittings	Bulb replacement

Power Supply:

OPTION	MAINTENANCE
Individual metered connection	Report defects

Solid waste:

OPTION	MAINTENANCE
Household container	Collect household waste
Communal Masonry enclosure	Deposit household waste; avoid spilling waste
Employ local sweeper	Payment for services

Community Hall:

OPTION	MAINTENANCE
Existing building	Management, cleaning and repair
New building	Management, cleaning and repair
Renovation of existing building	Management, cleaning and repair
Extension of existing building	Management, cleaning and repair

NB. Management includes payment of service charges for water, power and local taxes.

Some factors affecting levels of service

We can think of the different technical options listed in Table T6.1 as offering different *levels of service*. For example, the individual water connection or latrine offers the user a higher level of service than a water point or latrine which is shared with other users. Table T6.2 lists some specific points which will help you to focus on the key issues in relation to levels of service during the meetings with users when you are trying to find out what people want.

Table 6.2. Factors affecting levels of service by sector	
Sector	**Factors which affect level of service**
Water Supply	■ individual household connection ■ communal user group connection
Sanitation	■ individual household latrine ■ user group shared latrine
Drainage	■ extent of drainage systems ■ type of drains (e.g. open channel, road-as-drain) ■ materials of construction
Flood protection	■ extent of flood protection determined by retaining wall height
Access and paving	■ increase in access widths ■ extent of all-weather access ■ type of paving ■ type of traffic using the road
Security lighting	■ number of security lights ■ type of lantern
Power supply	■ individual connections
Solid waste management	■ individual household collection ■ communal user group collection
Community Buildings	■ plinth area ■ materials of construction

Calculating the costs of options and levels of service

In practice, users make choices about the services they want by balancing the perceived benefits against the costs incurred by them. They must therefore be aware of all of the costs involved when making a choice. The costs are made up of several components:

- capital costs of construction or taking a service connection (for example, water and power utilities or the municipality may have standard charges for making an individual user connection);

- operating costs, which cover the monthly charges payable to the water and power utilities or the municipality, including property taxes; and

- maintenance costs to make repairs in order to keep the facilities in good working order; in some but not all cases the maintenance costs will be covered by the monthly charges.

In order for users to make choices about levels of service, they must have information about the relative costs. What is required is an *indicative unit cost* for each of the options. This is dealt with in Section 5 of this manual on Programme implementation which describes the use of standard engineering details. Essentially, these give unit costs for different items of infrastructure. For example, if a particular type of paving costs so much per square metre to construct it is relatively simple to work out the cost of paving a known area. It becomes relatively simple and quick for the Programme engineers to give residents and service users indicative costs to assist them in decision making. This is easily built into a spreadsheet.

Note that it is essential that the approach to cost estimating is mechanised through the use of spreadsheets. Users are being asked complex questions about both the relative priority they attach to the different services and to different levels of service within each sector. This can generate a large number of possibilities for every user group; without this form of automation, it is impossible to turn round the cost estimation in a realistic time. See Tools 15 and 16 associated with Section 5.

References

Cotton A.P. and Franceys R.W.A.,(1991) *Services for Shelter*, Liverpool Planning Manual 3, Liverpool University Press.

Tool 7 User demand for service improvements

How this tool will help you

'Demand' is about finding out what people actually want and the extent to which they are prepared to commit the resources at their disposal. This tool will help you to carry out the three related activities (see Section 3a, Table 3a.1) in the Framework for local action planning:

- assess users priorities and demand;
- review costs; and
- reassess user priorities and demand.

Remember that you have already gathered useful information on user demand using participatory methods through your work on *Users perceptions of existing services* (Tool 5). We now build on this earlier work to help you to find out more about:

- the relative demand for different services;
- the need to actively stimulate demand for certain services such as sanitation; and
- using what people already pay as an indicator of demand for different levels of service.

Using this tool

The activities relating to demand assessment described in this tool need to be carried out in a participatory way with the service users. See Tools 1, 2 and 3 for further guidance. It is likely that a range of techniques will be required, and this will need the support of skilled facilitators; NGOs may have an important role to play in assisting you here.

As part of the preparation for this work, it is crucial to make sure that all of the team including external facilitators understand what we refer to and describe below as the 'financial rules of the game' for the upgrading programme (see below in *Who pays for what*). If you carry out the work on assessing the relative demand for different services and on assessing what people already pay, this will lead you to clear inputs to the Local Action Plan.

Also included at the end of this tool is a section on promoting the demand for services. This is particularly relevant to sanitation and is a longer term issue which may merit a separate programme component.

For further information and guidance on aspects of willingness to pay see the DFID *Guidance Manual on Water Supply and Sanitation Programmes* p39 (WELL 1998) for a summary of techniques.

Who pays for what?

The information about the relative costs of different components of infrastructure and different levels of service is at the centre of the discussions and negotiations about demand. The real issue is where the money comes from and in the case of grant or loan funding, what restrictions there are on spending it. There are a number of possibilities:

- service users pay all of the costs themselves;
- matching grants where an agency puts up the same amount as, or a fixed percentage of, the service users contribution;
- there is a local development budget for a particular area which can be allocated according to the collective decision of the local residents/service users; and
- restrictions are placed on the way in which the local development budget can be used in order to satisfy objectives of the funding institution; how much user choice is there?

There are therefore important choices to be made. For example:

- are some householders willing to pay the full cost for installing individual connections and pay the monthly tariff?
- how much of the available development budget are user groups and the wider community willing to allocate to improving specific services?

These issues are at the centre of the following discussions on demand which you will have with residents. It is clearly essential that indicative costs for possible options have been estimated as outlined in Tool 6.

It is essential that both the programme implementing team and the service users thoroughly understand what the 'financial rules of the game' are when embarking on these (or indeed any) types of demand assessment.

Relative demand for different services

Assessing the demand for improved services in urban upgrading programmes is not an easy matter. Firstly, you need to assess the relative priority which people put on the different services:

- water supply;
- sanitation;
- drainage;
- flood protection;
- access and paving;
- power and security lighting;
- solid waste management; and
- community buildings.

This can be quite difficult to assess, particularly where user groups are likely to be involved and where the services are 'common', such as storm drainage. A variety of the participatory techniques described in Tools 1 and 2 need to be used, but the key point is that there needs to be some way of confining the discussions to that which is realistic so that people are able to trade off the perceived benefits of one service with those of another. This is where the indicative costs and sources of finance are crucially important:

- how much will a particular option cost?;
- where is the money coming from: if there is a local development budget, how much is available and what are the restrictions on its use?

Secondly, there are issues about different levels of service, for example whether to pay extra for a house connection rather than a shared service. There is also the possibility that particular user groups wish to take higher service levels.

If individual households want to pay for individual service connections using their own resources, this is relatively straightforward and can be negotiated directly with the service provider. Matters become more complicated when users have to express their priorities for different services and to apportion a development budget across different service sectors.

What do people pay for existing services?

When outsiders visit urban poor areas, they often get the impression that services are totally lacking. This is rarely the case. Residents have often invested their own resources to try to make things better; they may pay significant amounts of money (in relation to their family income) to obtain water from private taps and to use latrines. These are the costs which poor people pay in order to cope; they may be paying a high price for a poor service.

Assessing how much people already pay to access services is a very useful starting point in dealing with user priorities and demand, as it gives an indication of peoples' willingness to pay. A checklist is provided in Table T7.1. The point is that households may spend quite a large proportion of their income accessing poor quality services. The upgrading programme has the potential to deliver much improved services, but these must be pitched at a level which people are willing to pay for.

Table T7.1. Assessing what people already pay	
Activity Checklist	**Findings**
How much capital cost have families already invested in services both on their plot, amongst a group of other users and in the community at large for the following: ■ water ■ sanitation ■ access & paving ■ protecting their dwellings from flooding ■ drainage ■ solid waste removal ■ power & security lighting ■ community buildings	
How much do people pay in recurrent cost for accessing and maintaining those services. This applies particularly to water supply, power supply and sanitation.	

The information you obtain about what people already pay is very useful; in your discussions about priorities and levels of service with service users, it helps you to match up the likely costs of different options with the 'price range' which users are already used to and can sustain. Of course, they may want to spend either more or less. This is particularly important with regard to the recurrent costs for operation and maintenance. The capital costs may come from the development budget, but the recurrent costs (at least) must be paid for by the users, and the information on what people already pay is useful in matching up service levels on the basis of sustaining recurrent costs.

Output from user demand investigations

The outcome of these discussions with users has to be transformed into specific proposals to be included in the Local Action Plan. Table T7.2 gives examples of the sort of practical details which are needed; if you keep these in mind during your meetings and discussions it will help you to keep a clear focus on the information that is needed.

Table T7.2. Examples of required inputs to Local Action Plans	
Sector	**Inputs to Local Action Plans**
Water Supply	■ number and location of individual connections ■ number and location of communal supply points ■ location and type of aprons and bathing enclosures ■ identification of specific user groups ■ location and capacity of water supply lines
Sanitation	■ number and location of individual household latrines ■ number and location of shared latrines ■ identification of specific user groups
Drainage	■ location, type and capacity of drains
Flood protection	■ location and height of retaining walls
Access & paving	■ location and type of paving ■ location and details of any revisions to access widths
Security lighting	■ number, type and location of security lights ■ location of power lines and ancillary equipment (transformers etc)

Table T7.2. (continued)	
Sector	**Inputs to Local Action Plans**
Power supply	■ location of individual connections
Solid waste management	■ individual household collection ■ communal user group collection ■ identification of specific user groups
Community Buildings	■ location ■ plinth area ■ materials of construction

Converging on a solution

Having used participatory techniques to assess peoples' priorities for services and what they already pay, you are now in a position to discuss possible improvements to the various services. Agree a preliminary list of improvements and proceed to the next stage in the Framework (refer back to Table 3a.1) which is to explore technical options which can satisfy these initial demands expressed by the users. The framework leads you through the process whereby you estimate costs for the initial proposals, discuss these with the users and then modify the original proposals accordingly.

There can be important demonstration effect whereby demand develops during and after implementation; people see the advantages and benefits of certain service improvements when they are in place with others using them. This is where a demand based approach becomes particularly difficult to manage where external finance is involved; it is difficult to reconcile this with conventional spending programmes which have prescribed physical and financial targets. This indicates the need for greater flexibility to accommodate such growth in demand.

Stimulating demand by active promotion

In parts of South Asia, one of the problems is that people do not necessarily perceive sanitation to be a priority. The approach adopted in this manual for developing the Local Action Plan is very much 'demand led'; in other words, we are responding to what people want and not telling them what they should have. However, if the objectives of an urban upgrading programme involve improvements to health and environmental conditions, whether it brings direct funding of improvement works or not, then sanitation is a key component. If it is omitted because there is no obvious 'user demand', then at least some of the objectives and benefits of the upgrading programme will not be achieved.

It has also been found that just providing latrines for people does not necessarily work; people must use them, keep them clean and well-maintained and develop improved hygiene behaviour practices if the benefits are to be fully realised. Therefore we need to adopt a different approach whose purpose is to **promote the importance of sanitation**. This means that we need to develop methods which explain and convince people of the importance of sanitation, and hence of acquiring and maintaining a latrine. The methods currently being developed are called social marketing techniques; these focus on the user in a way which is similar to the way commercial organisations try to get consumers to buy their goods and products. There are several important implications of adopting a promotional approach in order to stimulate demand for sanitation (or other services):

- there is a long and unpredictable lead time involved in developing activities and seeing success materialise;

- similarly, because the approach aims to generate demand, it is not possible to specify how many latrines will exist on the ground after a fixed period of time; this obviously is totally dependent on the success of the promotional activities.

A detailed discussion of social marketing for hygiene and sanitation promotion is beyond the scope of this manual. For more details please refer to the DFID Guidance Manual on Water Supply and Sanitation Programmes (WELL 1998): Section 2.3 *Health Aspects* and Section 2.8 *A Social Marketing Approach to Hygiene Promotion and Sanitation Promotion*

References

WELL, (1998) *Guidance Manual on Water Supply and Sanitation Programmes*

SERVICES FOR THE URBAN POOR

Tool 8 Gender issues

How this tool will help you

Gender is a 'cross cutting' issue; this means that it has to be considered at all stages of the planning process and is not something that can be dealt with on a discrete basis and 'ticked off' as a specific activity. This tool gives examples of issues related to services which are likely to be particularly important for women. However, it very important not just to treat gender through a 'check-list approach'; field teams must be sensitive to the fact that men and women have different priorities and needs which need to be picked up during discussions and meetings.

See also Tool 2 Participatory information gathering.

Using this tool

Table T8.1 presents some of the key points in relation to the various technical options which have a particular gender dimension and which should be taken into account. This relates to the central role which women play in accessing and providing different services for their families. It should also include specific features in the design and specification which may deviate from standard engineering details if necessary.

Table 8.1. Possible gender–related issues by sector

Sector	Possible gender–related issues
Water Supply	■ design features of communal supply points and bathing enclosures to ensure privacy ■ walking distance to supply points and bathing enclosures
Sanitation	■ need for separate male/female cubicles for shared latrines ■ location of shared latrines ■ superstructure details: ventilation, lighting, door details
Drainage	■ sullage drain connections

Table 8.1. (continued)

Sector	Possible gender–related issues
Flood protection	■ extent of flood protection works to minimise domestic disruption due to flooding
Access and paving	■ location of all-weather paved areas as these are used for a wide variety of household and income generating activities
Security lighting	■ location of lanterns to improve personal safety and encourage use of facilities such as latrines and community buildings outside daylight hours
Power supply	■ individual household issue
Solid waste management	■ women are the managers of household waste, involved in resale and reuse activities, carrying waste to bins, and the employment of local sweepers
Community buildings	■ space available appropriate for important activities such as health clinics, pre-school groups, and income generating activities

For further information and guidance on gender issues, please refer to the DFID *Guidance Manual on Water Supply and Sanitation Programmes* (WELL 1998): Section 2.2 *Social Development Perspectives;* sub section 2.2.4 contains more specific details.

References

WELL, (1998) *Guidance Manual on Water Supply and Sanitation Programmes*

Tool 9 Formation of user groups

How this tool will help you

This tool will help you to carry out the following activities in the Framework for local action planning (see Table 3a.1, Section 3a):

- discuss operation & maintenance requirements;
- assess users priorities and demand; and
- reassess users priorities and demand.

User groups are clearly central to the successful operation of the services after implementation. This tool will help you to define the user groups for services; it goes through some of the problems of dealing with communal services and provides a checklist of factors to consider for each service sector.

Using this tool

In your discussions with the service users, it is essential to establish which households will use which facilities; this is described in the section *Why we need user groups*. This is yet another complex issue, but you will find that it begins to emerge as a result of your work with the users concerning the assessment of priorities and demand, and about O&M requirements. Use the checklist of issues in Table T9.1 to help you to take account of the most important problems which may arise in each service sector.

Why we need user groups

For services which are provided to individual households, the responsibility for operation, maintenance, and general care of the facilities rests with the household concerned. This is much less clear for facilities such as public standposts, 'communal' latrines, and communal waste bins. Theoretically they belong to everybody in 'the community', but the reality is usually that they belong to nobody; there is no real sense of ownership, they are not looked after, maintenance is very poor, and they can rapidly fall into disrepair.

Nevertheless, it is simply not practical for everyone to have individual household services; some facilities will need to be provided on a communal basis.

The most important point here is that a group of users for any facility can be clearly identified. We can think of facilities being *shared*, implying a restricted number of users, rather than *communal*, which in practice has come to mean use by everybody.

Working with a clearly defined user group from the outset can help in the following ways:

- increasing the chances of cost recovery, because the user group is responsible for at least the costs of operating and maintaining the facility;
- promoting a sense ownership and greater care of the facility; and
- increasing the chances of the users carrying out cleaning and minor repairs.

This idea of shared facilities has a very important implication in relation to *demand*. The number and location of, for example, shared water supply points is determined through the identification of clear user groups. User groups do not have to be a standard size. They can come together on the basis of living close together, or on ties of kinship (which may be important for shared latrines). There may be existing neighbourhood groups of one sort or another which can also form the basis for user groups. This is completely different from the traditional approach of following standards and norms such as 200 users per tap and a maximum walking distance of 150 metres regardless of the views of the users. We may have more taps than specified by traditional norms.

Table T9.1 considers some issues in relation to user groups by sector which you can explore in discussions. Care needs to be taken here; small lanes and housing clusters are apparently obvious ways to define user groups, but there are cases where the social interactions between households make it complex. Establishing user groups for shared latrines can be particularly sensitive in this respect.

User groups will need strengthening; this is an area where local NGOs may be able to provide essential support.

Table T9.1. User group issues by sector

Sector	User group issues
Water Supply	■ location of handpumps and/or standposts, bathing enclosures, washing aprons
Sanitation	■ shared latrines
Drainage	■ needs to be considered as a part of the total drainage system for the site and integrated with the surrounding area; there is rarely scope for more individual choices
Flood protection	■ some groups on the margins may be amongst the poorest who are particularly vulnerable; take care that they are not neglected
Access and paving	■ affects the immediate environment of the plot, and therefore tends to group neighbours in particular streets, lanes and clusters
Security lighting	■ location
Power supply	■ individual household issue
Solid waste management	■ location of shared waste bins
Community buildings	■ this is a wider issue which will affect the whole of the community in question

Tool 10 Cost recovery

How this tool will help you

This tool will help you to carry out the activities *Review costs* and *Cost recovery* in the Framework for local action planning (see Table 3a.1 in Section 3a).

We have already explored how much people are willing to pay (see Tool 7 *User demand for service improvements*). Cost recovery is about how to get contributions in money or in kind from service users to cover the O&M costs and some of the capital costs where appropriate. This tool provides a checklist of key questions about the mechanics of cost recovery.

Using this tool

So far, in your discussions with the users, you have focused on what their priorities are in relation to the costs of different service options. The outcome of this is likely to be a reasonably clear idea of what improvements they want and how they are to be financed; that is, who is paying for what. Use the checklist below to explore in more detail with the users how costs can be recovered and the money collected.

Cost recovery

Recovering some or all of the costs of service provision is necessary if the services are to be sustainable in the long term. Rather than consider cost recovery by sector, it is more appropriate to discuss this with the users by looking at the way in which services are delivered and the possible ways in which costs can be recovered.

Table T10.1. Issues to discuss about cost recovery

Users	Comments
Individual service connections	Paid for by the household concerned; there are standard charges for the connection, and monthly tariffs to be paid. These are based on either meter readings or are flat rate charges. The householder will normally pay the bills direct to the agency supplying the service.
Shared services	These present real difficulties. O&M costs need to be recovered, but the amount of capital cost to be recovered depends on the approach the programme adopted to financing. (See the section on Who pays for what? in Tool 7 User demand for service improvements). Possibilities are as follows. ■ The municipality or utility levies a charge for the facility such as the water supply point to cover the cost of delivering water and undertaking repair and maintenance; the difficulty here is that the municipality is not dealing with an individual, but a user group which is a 'collective' organisation. ■ The user group collects money to fund minor repairs if the municipality or utility will not undertake repair and maintenance. In this case, the likely cost per month to each user group of operating and maintaining the supply point needs to be estimated. These costs can be surprisingly small; the problem is to motivate and mobilise user groups.

If user groups are established and become the mechanism for collecting the payments for the costs incurred, you can use the checklist in Table T10.2 to explore how this might be done.

Table T10.2. Checklist for the mechanics of cost recovery

Issue	Finding
How is the money to be collected?	
Where is it to be kept?	
To whom is it paid?	

Section 3b

Preparing Action Plans for
Networked Services

Who should read this
- Senior local officials at town/city level, including: programme directors; programme component managers who are responsible for developing and implementing action plans for improving services for the poor in towns and cities.
- Senior technical support staff on attachment to the programme including NGOs and local/international consultants.
- Managers of other concerned line departments and their staff.

Objectives of this section
To propose a framework and supporting tools for developing Action Plans for networked infrastructure external to urban poor neighbourhoods in response to the demands of the Local Action Plans which in turn reflect the demands and priorities of service users in urban poor areas. This should be read in conjunction with Section 3a on local action planning and Section 3c on consensus building.

What this section tells you
Network Service Plans deal with the need to supply services through city wide networks in order to meet local demand as expressed in the Local Action Plans.

The **Municipal Ward** is the focus for developing Area Network Service Plans because it is often the focus for O&M activities and the base for local Councillors.

Co-ordination of Area Network Service Plans in each sector (water, drainage, power, solid waste collection, sewerage) is necessary to ensure that demands made on primary networks can be met. This could be done by a services coordinating committee for the town/city.

A **framework for networked services planning** is presented which comprises the following stages:

- establish contact
- find out what is there
- identify future plans
- assess likely additional demand
- assess the capacity of existing secondary and primary infrastructure
- identify shortfalls in capacity
- identify missing infrastructure links
- options for upgrading system capacity
- prepare indicative costs
- prepare draft Area Network Service Plans
- co-ordination of Area Network Service Plans at the town level

The following **supporting tools** are provided

- Initial groundwork (Tool 11)
- Components of infrastructure systems (Tool 12)
- Assessing system capacity (Tool 13)
- Preparing Area Network Service Plans (Tool 14)

The need for networked services planning

Networked services require supporting infrastructure which is external to the household and neighbourhood. These can be classified into 'feeder' and 'collector' networks. Examples of feeder networks include :

- piped water supply; and
- power supply.

Examples of collector networks include:

- main drainage;
- solid waste collection; and
- sewered sanitation.

The purpose of Network Service Plans is to assess the capacity of existing primary and secondary infrastructure in each sector, and to consider what increases to this capacity are necessary in order to meet the expected demand generated through local action planning. Note that this increase in capacity will be achieved mainly through improvement to O&M of the existing infrastructure along with the construction of some new works. Improving services at the local (tertiary) level directly affects the secondary and primary distribution/collection infrastructure and it is important that all components are adequately sized. No amount of increase in the size of tertiary mains will result in an improved service if the supply to the area is inadequate. Conversely, the full benefits of improvements in supply capacity will not be realised if the tertiary systems are inadequate.

This part of the action planning process is therefore about the practicalities of balancing demand for services at the local level with the supply capacity of the networked city systems. This must also include a realistic assessment of the extent to which the city wide systems are likely to be upgraded and extended. There is an important practical point to make here: it may not prove possible to satisfy all of the demand for services which are in the Local Action Plans. This is where the *consensus building* component of action planning comes to the fore; plans are of no use unless they are achievable.

Area networked services planning

What needs doing

The first stage in networked service action planning focuses on the Municipal Ward. One of the reasons for this is that Municipal Wards are often an important centre of action for certain basic O&M activities such as drain cleaning, street sweeping and collection of local taxes. Wards are the operational base for Councillors and are also a potential focal point for negotiating changes to Local Action Plans and determining responsibilities for carrying out O&M in the newly upgraded neighbourhoods.

The output of this stage is an Area Network Service Plan for the Ward which, depending upon the technical options used, could have the following distinct components:

- water supply;
- drainage;
- sewerage, if appropriate;
- solid waste management; and
- power supply.

Who does it

In developing the Area Network Service Plans you will need to involve officials of the appropriate agency. For example, there may be specialist line agencies for water and power, whilst the municipality deals with drainage and solid waste management. The Area Network Service Plan will in the main deal with secondary networks, but will also cover some parts of the primary networks. It is important to remember that the extent of particular infrastructure networks are determined by their 'command area'; these cross the administrative boundaries of municipal wards into Zones/Circles and to the town as a whole, especially the primary networks.

Coordinating Area Network Service Plans

What needs doing

In order to produce a Network Service Plan for the town, the various Area Network Service Plans need to be coordinated for each sector to ensure that the demands made on the primary networks which go beyond the limits of the individual area plans can be satisfied. This will be relatively simple for small towns but becomes more complicated for larger cities.

The output from this will be a Network Service Plan for each of the infrastructure sectors listed above. The activities include abstracting all of the proposed networked service improvements and marking them up on a base plan of the whole city. This needs to be done for each sector so that it provides an overview 'at a glance' of what is proposed. This also ensures that the improvements are compatible with the existing 'command areas': for example drainage needs to be dealt with on the basis of the overall catchment and drainage basins within the city; water supply may be managed on a zonal basis using different water sources.

Who does it

The obvious approach is to hand over the coordination and plan preparation according to the specific local institutional responsibilities as indicated above. The difficulty which arises with this approach is that the responsibility then rests with an institution which might have only a very limited interest in a demand responsive programme targeted at improving services for the urban poor.

This could be addressed by setting up a 'Services Coordinating Committee' of senior officials from the concerned line agencies and municipal departments. This can provide an opportunity for information sharing and reporting back on progress, which may subsequently affect the direction of the networked services planning.

Even so, strong management and leadership is required from the institution with lead responsibility for implementing the services improvement programme. Depending upon local institutional arrangements and the attitude of individual officials, the Engineering Manager for the services improvement programme needs to drive and manage the process. This involves getting the different institutions and departments to deliver their plans and then coordinating their respective outputs. The Services Coordinating Committee could play a useful role here. It also helps if clear terms of reference are prepared for the work which is required from these other institutions and departments. Tool 13 *Assessing system capacity* provides guidance on what is required for the different sectors.

Framework for action planning for networked services

Table 3b.1 presents the framework for action planning for networked services; it gives a brief description of each component and refers to the various tools which describe the components in more detail, and provide help with what to do.

Table 3b.1. Framework for action planning for networked services

Activity	Description	Further guidance
Establish contact	Make contact with: ■ key staff in relevant line departments of the munici-pality and in specialist line agencies e.g water, power supply ■ municipal councillors ■ offices of other politicians from the regional or national assemblies who may have development budgets under their control to introduce the ideas behind the programme for improving services ■ create a coordinating committee of officials from the agencies and the municipality.	
Find out what is there	■ Collect available maps and plans to locate existing infrastructure in each municipal Ward. ■ Identify proposed urban poor project areas in relation to existing primary & secondary infrastructure lines.	Tool 11 Initial groundwork
Identify future plans	■ Identify and collect detailed information from line departments and utilities on future plans for extending and upgrading infrastructure within the municipality, including maps and designs. ■ Identify how these proposed improvements affect those Wards in which upgrading is to take place.	Tool 11 Initial groundwork

Table 3b.1. (continued)

Activity	Description	Further guidance
Assess likely additional demand	The Local Action Plan for each community which is to be upgraded is the key source of information. ■ Abstract the assessments of the demand for improved services in each service sector. ■ Bring together these assessments for increased demand from each locality to be upgraded and from other new developments which can be identified in the Ward. This creates an overall picture for the Ward which forms a key part of the Area Network Service Plan.	
Assess the capacity of existing secondary and primary infra-structure	This is the key activity, which is both time consuming and complex. ■ Note that the users provide essential information; each Local Action Plan contains a section on user perceptions of how well existing services perform and where problems occur. ■ Visit the localities to be upgraded to undertake some survey work on infrastructure condition. ■ Carry out calculations to assess actual capacity.	Tool 13 Assessing system capacity Tool 12 Components of infrastruc-ture systems
Identify shortfalls in capacity	Identify potential supply problems in the secondary and primary infra-structure. Do this by comparing the assessments of existing capacity with the additional demands (see above).	Tool 13 Assessing system capacity Tool 12 Components of infrastruc-ture systems

Table 3b.1. (continued)

Activity	Description	Further guidance
Identify missing infrastructure links	Identify where there are missing infrastructure links (e.g. water supply pipelines, outfall drainage channels) between localities to be upgraded and existing infrastructure lines.	
Options for upgrading system capacity	Area Network Service Plans for each sector need to propose ways to overcome the shortfalls in capacity of the primary and secondary infrastructure in the light of existing future plans of line departments and utilities.	Tool 13 Assessing system capacity Tool 12 Components of infrastructure systems
Prepare indicative costs	These need to be split into costs associated with: ■ improving O&M ■ new construction.	Tool 16 Spreadsheets for cost estimation
Prepare draft Area Network Service Plans	These incorporate: ■ base plans identifying all relevant infrastructure in the area ■ assessment of existing capacity ■ identification of new demands ■ potential shortfalls in supply capacity ■ technical proposals for upgrading supply capacity to match expected demand ■ plans identifying proposed new infrastructure in the area ■ indicative costs of proposals.	Tool 14 Preparing Area Network Service Plans
Coordination of Area Network Service Plans at the town level	Bring the individual Area Network Service Plans together to identify proposals across the town or city. This draft becomes the basis for discussions and negotiation with the line departments and possibly higher levels of government and external donors. Particular issues are the feasibility and cost of increasing the capacity of primary and secondary infrastructure.	Tool 11 Initial groundwork Tool 13 Preparing Area Network Service Plans

Preparing the Area Network Service Plans

An Area Service Plan needs to be prepared for each Municipal Ward when service improvements proposed in the Local Action Plan link into the city networks for infrastructure and service delivery, as indicated in Table 3b.2.

Table 3b.2. Preparation of Area Network Service Plans by sector

Service Sector	Requirement for Area Network Service Plans
Water supply	Required only for piped supplies
Sanitation	Required only for sewered sanitation
Surface drainage	Required
Power and Security lighting	Required
Solid Waste Management	Required
Access and paving	Required only for improved access links
Community buildings	Not required

Table 3b.3 suggests a structure for what the Area Service Plans should contain.

Table 3b.3. Suggested contents of Area Network Service Plans

Section	Contents
Existing situation	Service plans which are marked up on copies of the baseplan (see Tool 11) covering the entire Ward which identify: ■ the location of primary and secondary infrastructure ■ the localities to be upgraded ■ any existing infrastructure links into the localities to be upgraded
Existing demands on infrastructure	■ specify the estimated existing demands/loadings on the primary and secondary infrastructure lines in the area (see Tool 13 for suggested calculation details) ■ mark these demands/loadings on copies of the service plans
Capacity of existing infrastructure	Estimate capacity of the primary and secondary infrastructure lines in the area: ■ water: pipelines, pumping stations, storage reservoirs

Table 3b.3. (continued)

Section	Contents
	■ drainage: channels, canals ■ sewerage: sewers, pumping stations ■ power: transmission lines, transformers These should be marked on the service plans
New demands on infrastructure	■ use the Local Action Plans for each of the neighbourhoods to be upgraded to obtain estimates of the expected new demands/loadings which needs to be supplied via the primary and secondary networks in each infrastructure sector ■ estimate the new total demands/loadings on the primary and secondary infrastructure lines in the area (see Tool 13 for suggested calculation details) ■ mark these demands/loadings on copies of the service plans
Identify capacity shortfall	This is the justification for uprating the primary and secondary systems. ■ compare the estimated capacity of the infrastructure lines and items of equipment with the required loading
Identify missing links	Determine required capacity and mark up on service plans
Proposals for improvements	List proposals for improvement in a Table, (see Tool 13 for suggested details); also identify them on a copy of the service plans for the area. These should be split into: ■ improvements to the O&M of existing infrastructure ■ proposals for new works including new links between the neighbourhoods and existing networked infrastructure
Cost estimates	Prepare a table of indicative costs against each proposal
Proposals for financing	Identify possible sources of finance for the works (see Section 3c)
Implementation	Prepare a workplan indicating which organisation and department is to be responsible for each item of work, with possible start and end dates (see Section 3c)

Tools to support networked services planning

The following tools have been developed to support the activities required to carry out networked services planning: you will find these in the following part of this section of the manual.

Tools to support Action Plans for Networked Services	
Tool	**Description**
11	Initial groundwork
12	Components of infrastructure systems
13	Assessing system capacity
14	Preparing Area Network Service Plans

Tool 11 Initial groundwork

How this tool will help you

This tool provides you with guidance on collecting and assembling the baseline information about the primary and secondary infrastructure which is already there, and on the preparation of further maps and plans which identify the proposals for improving this infrastructure. This is essential in order to prepare Area Network Service Plans for each Ward.

Using this tool

The first stage in preparing Area Network Service Plans is to collect as much information as possible about the local services. Note that it is particularly important to meet with all of the service providing agencies and departments to discuss what plans they might have to improve and extend the infrastructure. We also suggest where to look for this information; obviously local officials are best placed to advise on this. The checklists are grouped as follows:

- what information to collect (Table T11.1); and
- what to prepare from the information which has been gathered; this will be used in developing the Area Service Plans (Table T11.2).

In summary, there are two key outputs from the initial groundwork which are essential to the success of action planning for networked services:

- establishing contact with the different service providing agencies and setting up a coordinating committee; and
- preparation of master service drawings for each Ward which can be marked up with the existing infrastructure in each sector; the proposed infrastructure improvements are also marked up. This provides an 'at a glance' view of the Network Service Plans.

Table T11.1. Information gathering checklist	
Information to collect	**Suggestions on how to get the information**
City Plan showing Ward/ political boundaries	Available in Municipality.
Identify larger scale base plans covering each Ward; suitable scales are between 1:5000 and 1:10,000	Municipality, Urban Development Authority. Also Land Revenue Department may have suitable scale plans which can be updated.
Establish the precise institutional responsibilities for planning, construction and O&M of infrastructure by sector	It is essential to interview staff of all agencies, both at headquarters and in zonal or Ward offices. Remember that actual roles and responsibilities often differ from what the organogram of the agency says should happen.
Service plans showing existing secondary and primary infrastructure for water, sewerage, drainage, power	Available from line departments or utilities. Requires site visits to check for recent additions and upgrading.
Service plans showing future proposals and their time scale for extending infrastructure for water, sewerage, drainage, power	Most line departments and utilities have plans to expand their networks. It is essential to plan and carry out a detailed programme of interviews with key agency officials.
New areas earmarked for future development	Available from the Urban Development Authority and the Municipality. Remember to ask about possible developments by State and National authorities and industrial development corporations.
Preliminary population estimates for urban poor and other new project areas	This data is usually obtained as part of preliminary surveys during project preparation.

Table 11.2. Checklist of what to prepare

Items to prepare from information gathered

1. A definitive list of all identified urban poor project areas; although these will have been identified during project preparation, make sure each area has a unique serial number.

2. Prepare base plans for the area (this will normally be equivalent to a municipal Ward). Although these may already exist it is quite likely that there will only be old plans which require updating or redrawing to include the most recent developments. Draw base plans to a scale of about 1:5000; show all roads, topographical features, water courses etc.

3. Use these base plans to prepare master service drawings for each Ward indicating existing secondary and primary infrastructure facilities by sector. These will include details such as pipe and channel sizes, estimated capacities, and the location of plant such as power transformers and pumping stations.

4. Identify those areas earmarked for new development which are definitely likely to start up within the lifetime of the upgrading programme, say 5-7 years.

5. On a copy of the master service drawings, mark up proposed extensions to primary and secondary infrastructure by sector.

Tool 12 Components of infrastructure systems

How this tool will help you

Systems of primary and secondary infrastructure can be complicated; this tool lists the main components of infrastructure by sector which need to be considered in assessing supply capacity.

Using this tool

Before starting work on assessing the capacity of the existing infrastructure, refer to Tables T12.1 to T12.5 which describe the components. As you proceed with your subsequent work on assessing capacity use the Tables as checklists to ensure that you have considered all the relevant parts of the system.

Table T12.1. Main components of piped water supply systems

Component	Description
Production facilities	Intakes, water treatment works, tubewells.
Bulk supply mains	These carry water from production facilities to service reservoirs. They are only required where the source is remote from the supply area.
Service reservoir storage facilities	These allow variations in demand over the day to be balanced and may also provide some back-up capacity in the event of a break in supply.
Primary or trunk mains	These are intended to convey water in bulk from one part of the network to another. They will not normally be required where supply is from tubewells located at intervals throughout the supply area.
Secondary mains	These link tubewells, service reservoirs and trunk mains with service mains. They normally have diameters of 150mm or greater and are laid to form loops.
Tertiary or service mains	These are mains of 100mm diameter or less that distribute water locally. They are often branches rather than loops.
House and standpost connections	Typically 12-25mm diameter.

Table T12.2. Main components of drainage systems

Component	Description
Plot drains	These are small, shallow open channels (or pipes) which connect paved areas on the plot to the local tertiary drains; they often carry sullage from the kitchen.
Tertiary collector drains	These are usually roadside open channels which collect runoff locally from paved surfaces and sullage water from plots, unless a sewerage system exists or plots are large enough to accommodate soakage pits. In some cases overflows from septic tanks or pit latrines are discharged; this creates local environmental health hazards.
Storage ponds and tanks	Storage of drainage water has the effect of reducing the maximum flow which the actual drains have to carry during a storm. Flow through natural ponds has this effect; unfortunately there is rarely enough room to construct purpose made storage ponds.
Secondary collector drains	These link the tertiary to the primary, and are usually open channels about 1 metre wide.
Primary drains	Large open channels which form the 'spine' of the drainage network. The natural topography dictates the line of the primary drains; a town or city may have several independent drainage catchments as a result.
Receiving water	This is where the drained water is finally disposed of; usually a stream, river, pond, lake or the sea.

Table T12.3. Main components of sewerage systems

Component	Description
House sewers	These collect the household wastewater from flush toilets and sullage from kitchens and bathrooms; they are usually 100mm diameter pipes.
Tertiary collector sewers	These collect the flows directly from house sewers; they are usually 150mm or 250mm diameter pipes.
Secondary collector sewers	These link the tertiary to the primary.
Primary sewers	Large buried pipes, or sometimes open channels which form the 'spine' of the network. The natural topography dictates the line of the primary sewers; a town or city may have several independent sewerage catchments as a result.
Wastewater treatment	Some form of sewage treatment is essential to avoid environmental pollution of the receiving water.
Receiving water	This is where the treated sewage effluent is finally disposed of; usually a stream, river, pond, lake or the sea.

Table T12.4. Main components of solid waste management systems

Component	Description
Household or communal storage	Storage of waste in household or communal containers.
Selling waste	Householders sell waste which has a value (glass, metal, paper) to itinerant waste buyers.
Primary collection	Emptying of household or communal containers and removal of the waste using small vehicles (note that the term 'primary' is confusing with respect to the other infrastructure sectors).
Transfer	A designated location serving an area as large as a municipal Ward where the waste from primary collection is unloaded prior to reloading for longer distance transportation
Haulage	Transport of waste from transfer station to more distant waste disposal facilities.
Disposal	Adequate waste disposal is necessary, for example by sanitary landfill or localised neighbourhood composting.

Table T12.5. Main components of power and security lighting systems

Component	Description
Production	Power plants which feed into grids covering a much larger area than water supply systems.
Primary distribution mains	High voltage lines which carry electricity in three phases at high voltage to district sub-stations.
District sub-station	The voltage of the supply is stepped down via transformers before distribution to users.
Local distribution	Low voltage power lines taken from the sub-station to distribute power around the site; usually less than 200m long. Overhead lines are cheaper than buried cables.
House connection	Single connections from the local distributor to a power meter in the house, from where power is distributed internally.

Tool 13 Assessing system capacity

How this tool will help you

In this tool, we provide guidelines for assessing whether there is adequate capacity in the secondary distribution and collection networks and in the local tertiary networks. You are also guided to the tools in Section 4 *Technical Guidelines* which deal with planning and design of services in more detail.

How to use this tool

Analysing system capacity is complicated and you need information about how the system works. You can do this by carrying out the following three activities.

1. **Use the Local Action Plans** to tell you how the services perform at the moment, and what the users perceptions of this performance are. You can abstract valuable information from these plans to guide you on where there are gaps in the supply systems.

2. **Look for simple things:** you can improve your understanding of the findings from Local Action Plans by going to sites, observing what is happening, making a few measurements and asking further questions. This needs to be done by a team with a good mix of technical and social skills.

3. **Carry out calculations** to determine the theoretical capacity of the systems and the new demands which they will have to deal with as a result of increased demands. The information obtained from the two previous stages helps you to identify what needs to be calculated. Section 4 *Technical Guidelines* tells you how to do the necessary calculations.

The material in this tool is presented in turn for each of the main infrastructure sectors.

Checklist for existing situation for drainage

Notes on how to use Table T13.1

- Column 1 tells you the sources of information
- Column 2 tells you what you can find out from these sources of information
- Column 3 states what this actually tells you about the problem
- Column 4 advises you as to the next steps you should take as a result of what you have found out
- Column 5 directs you to the tools in Section 4 of the manual on Technical Guidelines

Table T13.1. Checklist for existing situation for drainage

Source	What to find out	What it tells us	Action and outcome	Further guidance
From Local Action Plans	1. Existing and future areas to be drained	1. Basis for estimating loading on drainage systems	1. Input to local and area network system design	1. See point 9
	2. Location of flooding and low lying areas	2. Where the problems are concentrated	2. Input to local action plans: possible need for local landfill	
	3. Frequency of flooding in particular areas	3. Magnitude of the problem, and possible problems off site due to inadequate secondary system	3. Input to Local and Area Network Service plan	3. See point 9
	4. Where does water drain to after a storm	4. Natural drainage paths	4. Input to Local Action Plans: location of possible new drains and outfall points	
	5. What problems there are with blockage of existing drains	5. Possible causes of blockage and drainage problems; inadequate maintenance	5. Input to Local and Area Network Service Plans: roles & responsibilities for drain cleaning; discuss with Operations Dept.	5. Refer to solid waste management checklist

Table T13.1. (continued)

Source	What to find out	What it tells us	Action and outcome	Further guidance
From site inspection and interviews	6. Physical condition of the outfall points, any obstructions or restrictions to flow	6. Many problems with drainage result from downstream conditions	6. Input to Local Action Plan: minor improvements to outfall can significantly improve performance.	
	7. Water levels in outfall drains and relative bed levels of tertiary and secondary drains at outfall point	7. This determines the water levels in the tertiary drainage system	7. Input to calculation of water levels in drains	7. See points 11 & 14
	8. Extent of silting	8. Blockages further downstream or gradient of drain not steep enough or inadequate maintenance	8. Input to Local and Area Service Plans: cleaning and/or regrading of some drains	
By calculation	9. Runoff from existing tertiary area when upgraded	9. Loading on tertiary and secondary drains	9. Input to local and area network system design	9. See point 13
	10. Capacity of existing tertiary drains	10. Adequacy of existing tertiary drains; need for new, or enlargement of existing, drains	10. Include details in Local Action Plan	

Table T13.1. (continued)

Source	What to find out	What it tells us	Action and outcome	Further guidance
By calculation	11. Design of new or uprated tertiary drains to cope with new loading	11. Local network design	11. Include details in Local Action Plan	11. Tool D3
	12. Capacity of existing secondary drains	12. Adequacy of existing secondary drains; need for new, or enlargement of existing, drains	12. Input to Area Network Service Plan	12. Tools D2 and D3
	13. Design of additional or redesign of existing secondary drains for new loadings	13. Area network design	13. Input to Area Network Service Plan	13. Tool D3
	14. Hydraulic profiles in secondary drains	14. Determination of invert levels for tertiary drains at outfall into secondary drain (new or reconstructed)	14. Input to Local Action Plan and Area Network Service Plan	14. Tool D3

Doing the calculations

Table T13.2. tells you where you can find details about how to actually carry out the designs and calculations which are referred to in Table T13.1. These tools and handy tips are in Section 4 of the manual.

Table T13.2. Tools for further guidance	
Tool	**Guidance on**
D1	Drainage: objectives and options
D2	Drainage: planning
D3	Drainage: design
D4	Drainage: handy tips on where to use, construction and O&M

Checklist for existing situation for water supply

Notes on how to use Table T13.3.

- Column 1 tells you the sources of information

- Column 2 tells you what you can find out from these sources of information

- Column 3 states what this actually tells you about the problem

- Column 4 advises you as to the next steps you should take as a result of what you have found out

- Column 5 directs you to the tools in Section 4 of the manual on Technical Guidelines

Table T13.3. Checklist for existing situation for water supply

Source	What to find out	What it tells us	Action and outcome	Further guidance
From Local Action Plans	1. Future water demand	1. Required flow rates within the system and location of demands	1. Input to local and area network system design	1. See point 10
	2. No. of supply hours per day at present	2. Is there enough water in the system? Problems with bulk supply and possibly service reservoir storage	2. Input to Area Network Service Plans: discuss increasing supply hours with Operations Dept.	
	3. Seasonal reliability of non-piped supplies	3. Need for new or upgraded piped supply to supplement existing sources	3. Input to local and area network system design	
	4. Quality and potability of water	4. Users perceptions may be reflected in demand	4. Input to Area Network Service Plans: review problems with operations department	

Table T13.3. (continued)

Source	What to find out	What it tells us	Action and outcome	Further guidance
From site inspections and interviews	5. Measure residual pressure at taps	5. If less than 5m, too low; either tertiary or secondary or both distribution systems are inadequate	5. Calculate headloss in tertiary systems	5. See point 10
	6. Measure pressure at or near take off from secondary main	6. If less than 8-10m too low; secondary mains are inadequate	6. Calculate headloss in secondary main	6. See point 12
	7. Interruptions to supply from bursts & other system failures such as pumping	7. Problems with O&M of network	7. Input to Area Network Service Plans: discuss targeting investments with Operations Dept	
	8. Existing pumping capacity into local secondary mains	8. Adequacy of existing pumping systems	8. Check against requirements for new demand	8. See point 14; Tool W2
	9. Existing service reservoir storage capacity	9. Adequacy of storage to balance daily variations in demand	9. Check against requirements for new demand	9. See point 14; Tool W2

Table T13.3. (continued)

Source	What to find out	What it tells us	Action and outcome	Further guidance
By calculation	10. Head loss along existing tertiary network pipes using new demand when upgraded	10. Adequacy of existing pipeline capacity	10. Input to point 11	10. Tool W3
	11. Design of new or uprated tertiary pipelines to cope with new demand	11. Local network design	11. Input to Local Action Plan	11. Tool W3
	12. Headloss along secondary mains under new water demand	12. Adequacy of existing pipeline capacity	12. Input to point 13	12. Tool W3
	13. Design of new or uprated second-ary pipelines	13. Secondary network design	13. Input to Area Network Service Plan	13. Tool W3
	14. New pumping and storage requirements	14. Investigate how best to balance out increased pumping with increased storage	14. Input to Area Network Service Plan	14. Tool W2

Doing the calculations

Table T13.4. tells you where you can find details about how to actually carry out the designs and calculations which are referred to in Table T13.3. These tools and handy tips are in Section 4 of the manual.

Table T13.4. Tools for further guidance	
Tool	**Guidance on**
W1	Water supply: objectives and options
W2	Water supply: planning
W3	Water supply: design
W4	Water supply: handy tips on where to use, construction and O&M

Checklist for existing situation for sewerage

Notes on how to use Table T13.5

- Column 1 tells you the sources of information

- Column 2 tells you what you can find out from these sources of information

- Column 3 states what this actually tells you about the problem

- Column 4 advises you as to the next steps you should take as a result of what you have found out

- Column 5 directs you to the relevant tool in Section 4 of the manual on Technical Guidelines

Table T13.5. Checklist for existing situation for sewerage

Source	What to find out	What it tells us	Action and outcome	Further guidance
From Local Action Plans	1. Existing and future sewer connections	1. Basis for estimating loading on sewerage systems	1. Input to local and area network system design	
	2. Frequency of sewage backing up: overflowing manholes and/or toilets which won't flush properly some of the time	2. Local blockages or possible problems off site due to inadequate secondary system including lack of pumping capacity	2. Input to Local and Area Network Service Plans: explore operation of local sewage pumping stations	2. See point 6
	3. Location and frequency of sewer blockage	3. Identifies problem areas in tertiary system	3. Input to Local Action Plan for remedial works to remove local blockages	

Table T13.5. (continued)

Source	What to find out	What it tells us	Action and outcome	Further guidance
From site inspection and interviews	4. Sewage levels in secondary sewer and relative invert levels of tertiary and secondary sewers at outfall point	4. This determines the sewage flow levels in the tertiary sewerage system	4. Calculate 'water' level of sewage in tertiary sewers	4. See points 8 & 11
	5. Missing or damaged manhole covers	5. The most common way in which solid matter gets into sewers and blocks them	5. Input to Local Action Plan: replace covers and explore the cause of the problem	
By calculation	6. Outflow from existing tertiary area when upgraded	6. Loading on tertiary and secondary sewers	6. Input to local and area networked systems design	6. Tool S5
	7. Capacity of existing tertiary sewers	7. Adequacy of existing tertiary sewers; need for new sewers	7. Include details in Local Action Plan	7. Tools S4 and S5
	8. Design of new or redesign of existing tertiary sewers for new loading	8. Local network design	8. Include details in Local Action Plan	8. Tools S4 and S5

Table T13.5. (continued)

Source	What to find out	What it tells us	Action and outcome	Further guidance
By calculation	9. Capacity of existing secondary sewers	9. Adequacy of existing secondary sewers	9. Include details in Area Network Service Plans	9. Tool S5
	10. Design of additional or redesign of existing sewers for new loadings	10. Area network design	10. Include details in Area Network Service Plans	10. Tool S5
	11. Hydraulic profiles: relative water levels and invert levels of outfall sewer and tertiary sewers	11. Important effect on how well the system will operate. Determination of invert levels for tertiary sewers at outfall into secondary sewer (new or reconstructed)	11. Input to Local Action Plan and Area Network Service Plan	11. Tool S5

Doing the calculations

Table T13.6. tells you where you can find details about how to actually carry out the designs and calculations which are referred to in Table T13.5 . These tools and handy tips are in Section 4 of the manual.

Table T13.6. Tools for further guidance	
Tool	**Guidance on**
S1	Sanitation: objectives and options
S4	Sanitation: sewerage planning
S5	Sanitation: sewerage design
S6	Sewerage: handy tips on where to use, construction and O&M

Checklist for existing situation for power supply

Notes on how to use Table T13.7

- Column 1 tells you the sources of information

- Column 2 tells you what you can find out from these sources of information

- Column 3 states what this actually tells you about the problem

- Column 4 advises you as to the next steps you should take as a result of what you have found out

- Column 5 directs you to the tools in Section 4 of the manual on Technical Guidelines

Table T13.7. Checklist for existing situation for power supply

Source	What to find out	What it tells us	Action and outcome	Further guidance
From Local Action Plans	1. Existing and future demand	1. Power load requirements within the system	1. Input to local and area networked system design	1. See point 6
	2. No. of supply hours per day	2. Insufficient power available; possible problems with primary distribution	2. Input to Area Network Service Plans: discuss increasing supply hours with Operations Dept.	
From site inspections and interviews	3. Voltage at end of local distributor lines	3. If less than operating requirement either local distributor line is too long or the demand on the transformer is too large or both	3. Calculate transmission losses	3. See point 10
	4. Distance to local step down transformer	4. Check within recommended limits; maybe too far away for local distributor lines to maintain voltage	4. Input to local and area networked system design: discuss additional 3 phase supply and transformers	4. See points 7&10

Table T13.7. continued

Source	What to find out	What it tells us	Action and outcome	Further guidance
From site inspections and interviews	5. Interruptions to supply from system equipment breakdown	5. Problems with O&M of network	5. Input to Area Network Service Plans: discuss targeting investments with Operations Dept.	
By calculation	6. Transmission losses along tertiary lines using new demand when upgraded	6. Adequacy of existing transmission lines	6. Input to point 7	6. Tool P3
	7. Design of new or uprated power lines to cope with new demand	7. Local network design	7. Input to Local Action Plan	7. Tool P3
	8. Transmission losses along main supply lines using new demand	8. Adequacy of existing transmission lines	8. Input to point 9	8. Tool P3
	9. Design of additional main supply lines	9. Secondary network design	9. Input to Area Network Service Plan	9. Tool P3
	10. Requirements for additional step-down transformers	10. Secondary network design	10. Input to Area Network Service Plan	10. Tools P2 and P3

Doing the calculations

Table T13.8. tells you where you can find details about how to actually carry out the designs and calculations which are referred to in Table T13.7. These tools and handy tips are in Section 4 of the manual.

Table T13.8. Tools for further guidance	
Tool	Guidance on
L1	Power supply & lighting: objectives and options
L2	Power supply & lighting: planning
L3	Power supply & lighting: design
L4	Power supply & lighting: handy tips on where to use, construction and O&M

Checklist for existing situation for solid waste management

Notes on how to use Table T13.9:

- Column 1 tells you the sources of information

- Column 2 tells you what you can find out from these sources of information

- Column 3 states what this actually tells you about the problem

- Column 4 advises you as to the next steps you should take as a result of what you have found out

- Column 5 directs you to the tools in Section 4 of the manual on Technical Guidelines

Table 13.9. Checklist for existing situation for solid waste management

Source	What to find out	What it tells us	Action and outcome	Further guidance
From Local Action Plans	1. Collection frequency	1. If less than once per week, service is inadequate	1. Input to Area Network Service Plans; discuss improvements at Ward level	
	2. Location of communal containers	2. If more than 50 metres from houses, unlikely to be used	2. Input to tertiary design; improve location of bins, and investigate option of household collection using privately engaged sweepers	2. Tool SW3
	3. Location of transfer points	3. Accessibility of transfer point by collection vehicles	3. Input to Area Network Service Plans	3. Tool SW1
From site inspections and interviews	4. Visual appearance	4. Attitude of residents towards clean environment	4. Consider need for awareness raising on clean environment issues	4. See Tool 7, section on 'Stimulating demand by active promotion'
	5. Drain blockage by solid waste	5. Poor solid waste management is causing problems with the drainage system	5. Input to Local and Area Network Service Plans; discuss at local and ward level	

Table 13.9. (continued)

Source	What to find out	What it tells us	Action and outcome	Further guidance
Operational: Ward office	6. Availability of municipal staff 7. Availability of vehicles for collecting waste from transfer points 8. Availability of other simple equipment	6. - 8. Resources available for use in the area	6. - 8. Input to Area Network Service Plans: need to negotiate at the Ward level to determine how best the existing resources can be allocated	6. - 8. Tools SW2 and SW3

Doing the calculations

Table T13.10. tells you where you can find details about how to actually carry out the designs and calculations which are referred to in Table T13.9 . These tools and handy tips are in Section 4 of the manual.

Table T13.10. Tools for further guidance	
Tool	Guidance on
SW1	Solid waste management: objectives and options
SW2	Solid waste management: planning
SW3	Solid waste management: local initiatives

Tool 14 Preparing Area Network Service Plans

How this tool will help you

This tool helps you to prepare that part of the Area Network Service Plans which deal with the proposals for improvements to the primary and secondary infrastructure. It is based on the outcome of using Tool 13, which provides guidance on assessing the capacity of infrastructure systems to deliver services both at the local (tertiary) and area (secondary) levels under existing and future planned conditions. This tool abstracts the key points from Tool 13 which relate to the preparation of Area Network Service Plans.

How to use this tool

Your proposals for improvements need to summarise the findings of Tool 13 in a clear and concise way. Table 14.1 picks up the key findings from Tool 13 by service sector. You should provide answers to these questions as far as is possible; you can use these answers as the inputs into the proposals for improvement section of the Area Network Service Plans.

Many of the questions will have quite clear answers, where you can specify technical details such as the size and location of new pipe runs or channels. However, you will not have definite answers to a number of important questions because there are some issues which will become the subject of discussions with the various line departments. For example, the Area Network Service Plan for water supply could include an action along the lines of *discuss changes to the operation of the local pumping station.* Similarly for drainage, it could include *discuss drain cleaning programme with Operations department.* It is important to realise that these issues need to be raised at the coordinating committee (see Table 3b.1, Framework) and then taken forward into the next stage of plan development, namely Consensus Building. Remember, just because we specify an action in the plan does not mean that it will automatically take place.

Table 14.1. Points to include in Area Network Service Plans

Sector	Input to Area Network Service Plans
Drainage	■ capacity of existing drainage infrastructure ■ required capacity of drainage infrastructure ■ discuss drain cleaning programme with Operations Dept. ■ any changes to secondary drains to allow for increased loading ■ details of additional drains or redesign of existing drains ■ relative invert levels and details at outfall points of tertiary drains (new or reconstructed)
Water supply	■ capacity of existing water supply infrastructure ■ required capacity of water supply infrastructure ■ any changes to local network storage and pumping to allow for increased demand ■ if supply hours are infrequent, discuss increasing supply hours with Operations Dept. ■ if there are interruptions to supply due to equipment failure, discuss targeting investments with Operations Dept. ■ amendments to secondary mains ■ amendments to pumping system ■ improvements to local storage and bulk supply
Sewerage	■ capacity of existing sewerage infrastructure ■ required capacity of sewerage infrastructure ■ details of additional sewers or redesign of existing sewers ■ relative invert levels and details at outfall points of tertiary sewers ■ discuss operation of local sewage pumping stations with Operations Dept. ■ discuss sewer cleaning programme with Operations Dept.
Power supply	■ capacity of existing power supply infrastructure ■ required capacity of power supply infrastructure ■ if supply hours are infrequent, discuss increasing supply hours with Operations Dept. ■ if there are interruptions to supply due to equipment failure, discuss targeting investments with Operations Dept. ■ amendments to secondary power lines ■ additional requirements for transformers
Solid waste management	■ additional transfer points ■ discuss improvements to local operations at Ward level for including: local waste collection frequency, operation of transfer stations, haulage and disposal

Section 3c

Consensus Building

Who should read this
- Senior local officials at town/city level, including: programme directors; programme component managers who are responsible for developing and implementing action plans for improving services for the poor in towns and cities.
- Senior technical support staff on attachment to the programme including NGOs and local/international consultants.
- Managers of other concerned line departments and their staff.

Objectives of this section
To describe why we need to bring key people (stakeholders) together to achieve a consensus on Local Action Plans and Action Plans for Networked Services, to propose what needs to be done and suggest possible ways of going about it in order to agree a way forward which leads to implementation of service improvements in poor areas.

What this section tells you
Arguably the most crucial issue in action planning is the need to bring people together to **negotiate the way forwards** and agree what is possible in the local context. The outcome is an agreed allocation of resources to implement particular aspects of the action plans.

Consensus building between user groups, local politicians and municipal and line agency officials has frequently been missing from technically driven planning processes in the past.

The following **activities** are amongst those requiring consensus:
- review current institutional priorities of service providers;

- review Area Network Service Plans;
- review the Co-ordinated Network Service Plan for the town/city;
- identify possible sources for capital financing;
- identify possible sources for financing improvements to O&M;
- agree criteria for prioritising proposals;
- prioritise the proposals using agreed criteria;
- review strategy for implementation;
- review detailed workplans: new capital works;
- review detailed workplans: service improvements through O&M; and
- evaluate the impact of these decisions on the Local Action Plans.

Consensus building for achieving **improved O&M** is a central issue.

The greatest challenge is to develop mechanisms for consensus building which ensure that **stakeholders meet on an equal basis**.

There are many potential **problems and pifalls** to be overcome:

- vested/delegated authority of committees and forums;
- need for strong positive leadership to bring together those who previously had no reason to meet;
- incentives to participate: stakeholders need to see that this will make a real difference;
- information sharing between professional and non-professional groups;
- dispute resolution; and
- increasing public awareness is an important wider role for consensus building.

Possible **mechanisms for consensus building** include Ward Committees, a Municipal Committee and forums open to the public at the Ward and Town levels.

Consensus building and the local context

We have stated previously that these action planning guidelines are most appropriate in a local context where:

- there is a commitment within municipal government to improve services for the poor which has higher level policy support from state/central government; and

- this policy supports a more decentralised approach to planning which accepts the importance of involving users in the process.

The extent to which these conditions exist is highly variable, yet without these 'policy drivers' it is very unlikely that the potential benefits from improved planning of services will be realised. There exist many situations in which a lot of preparatory work including local workshops will be required in order to convince local officials firstly of the importance of involving users in local planning and secondly in developing a more integrated approach to city wide planning. This is beyond the scope of this manual and we make reference to other work which deals with these issues. This section assumes that there is a higher level commitment to these overall aims and it focuses on looking for possible mechanisms which are workable given this policy support.

Consensus building: why we need to bring key people together

Sections 3a and 3b provided guidelines for developing:

- Local Action Plans for improvements to neighbourhood services; and
- Area Network Service Plans for improvements to the wider town/city level networked services which are required in order to support the Local Action Plans.

Again, we emphasise that planning involves more than a set of technically based activities; the success of any planning process is judged by evaluating what is actually done on the ground as a result of the planning. Having developed the above Action Plans, we now have to negotiate and agree what is possible with all of the concerned people ('stakeholders'). We use the term 'consensus building' to describe this process.

Consensus building has often been missing from technically-driven planning approaches in the past. The reason for bringing stakeholders together is that the Local Action Plans and the Area Network Service Plans are very closely linked. Wherever there are networked services, the success of the Local Plans depends upon which parts of the town/city level Network Service Plans are actually implemented. This applies to both construction of new works and improved operation and maintenance of existing infrastructure. To recap, networked services include:

- piped water supply;
- drainage;
- solid waste collection;

- power supply; and
- sewered sanitation.

Non-networked services at the neighbourhood and household level can be developed independently of municipal services through local action alone; these include:

- wells and handpumps;
- unsewered sanitation;
- local drainage to soakpits or ponds; and
- solid waste disposal in pits.

In practice it is rarely possible to deliver all of the required improvements to networked services at the town/city level to satisfy the demands expressed through the local plans. The costs of improving the primary and secondary infrastructure networks can be high and will benefit all of the citizens of the area, not just the urban poor.

Section 3b describes how plans are prepared for networked services at the Municipal Ward level. These are then co-ordinated to identify actions needed to improve the primary infrastructure networks for the town as a whole. Therefore, there is a need for consensus building at two levels:

- the Ward level, to prepare the Area Network Service Plans and agree which works will have priority; and
- the town/city level, where the specialist line agencies and municipal departments responsible for specific services prioritize which works to undertake in order to improve primary networks.

A mechanism is needed within which these negotiations can take place, involving: the various Municipal Departments; specialist line agencies; Councillors and other local politicians; representatives of service user groups and other key target groups. The outcome of the negotiations needs to be an agreement on allocation of resources, which will in turn affect what can be done in the Local Action Plans. This then requires both service providers and service users to modify their plans accordingly or explore other options. It is important to realise that the scope for upgrading bulk supply capacity may turn out to be very limited; this will limit options and choices for the Local Action Plans. Not everybody can or will be satisfied and compromises have to be made in order to move ahead.

What needs to be done

The consensus building process has two important components:

- information sharing between the various stakeholders; and
- advising the individuals and/or committees which have decision making authority.

Table 3c.1 proposes activities which need to be carried out as part of the consensus building process in order to arrive at a shared view amongst the various stakeholders about the best way forward for implementing Action Plans.

Table 3c.1. Activities requiring consensus	
Activity	**Brief description**
Review current institutional priorities of service providers	- establish the priority currently assigned by the concerned Departments and line agencies to particular network improvements including O&M - review their workplans for the coming years
Review Area Network Service Plans	These define the secondary infrastructure network needs including O&M at the Ward level for: - water distribution - power distribution - storm water collection - solid waste collection and transfer - sewerage
Review the Co-ordinated Network Service Plan for the town/city	This defines primary infrastructure network needs including O&M across the town as a whole looking at the: - bulk water supply and distribution to zones of the town - bulk power supply and distribution to zones of the town - main stormwater drainage - main sewerage and treatment - haulage and disposal of solid waste

Table 3c.1. (continued)	
Activity	**Brief description**
Identify possible sources for capital financing	Based on the estimated cost of the works, identify different sources of financing for capital works; for example: ■ existing budgets for capital works programmes ■ funds assigned to local, regional and national politicians for service improvements ■ special programme funds available at the state or national level including infrastructure funds and banks ■ donor funding through bilatertal aid and/or international lending banks ■ private sector lending agencies
Identify possible sources for financing improvements to O&M	Based on the estimated costs and staff requirements, identify different sources of financing; for example: ■ increase efficiency of revenue collection through billing more service users and collecting more of the bills already issued ■ potential to increase revenue for service delivery through increased property tax, cesses, service charges, betterment levies, and other means prescribed by local Statutes and Government Orders ■ more effective and efficient deployment of agency staff ■ potential role of the Mayor or other senior municipal officials in rationalising the distribution of local funds to optimise improvements
Agree criteria for prioritising proposals	These depend on the specific objectives of the upgrading programme and need to be established locally. The following are examples: for each particular proposed service improvement investigate: ■ how many of the target group of primary stakeholders stand to benefit ■ relative priority assigned by service users to improvements in a particular service sector ■ the cost per beneficiary ■ availability of and cost of finance ■ ease of undertaking works, e.g. problems of land ownership and acquisition ■ the probability of funds being available and the flexibility which agencies have to reallocate future finance

Table 3c.1. (continued)	
Activity	**Brief description**
Prioritise the proposals using agreed criteria	■ use these criteria to establish the priority list for the proposals ■ compare this with the current investment and service improvement priorities of the departments and agencies ■ negotiate changes to some of these current priorities in view of the priority list for works ■ the extent to which this can be done may be constrained by proposed sources of finance and the flexibility to reallocate planned funding for capital investment works ■ there is likely to be much more flexibility for service improvements which an be achieved through better O&M
Review strategy for implementation	Identify for both new capital works and improvements to O&M: ■ what can be done in the immediate future ■ what is medium term and what requirements need to be met in order to move ahead ■ what is long term because it is expensive/difficult and what requirements need to be met in order to move ahead
Review detailed workplans: new capital works	Request the concerned departments and agencies to prepare detailed workplans for schemes including time schedules: ■ technical survey and planning ■ drawing up detailed proposals ■ preparation of contract packages ■ letting of contracts or assignment of direct labour force ■ completion of contract

Table 3c.1. (continued)

Activity	Brief description
Review detailed workplans: service improvements through O&M	Request the concerned departments and agencies to prepare detailed workplans for the schemes including time schedules: ■ changes and improvements to supply hours for water and power ■ technical survey and planning for major tasks ■ drawing up detailed proposals for major tasks ■ re-assignment of direct labour for routine work ■ use of external contractors ■ ensure plans link to the agreed roles and responsibilities at the tertiary level as defined in the local Memorandums of Understanding
Evaluate the impact of these decisions on the Local Action Plans	The decisions on priorities have important 'knock-on' effects on the networked service components of Local Action Plans. ■ use the priority list of proposals to identify which Local Action Plans are adversely affected by the priorities ■ review with the local user groups how their Local Action Plans can be modified in this light ■ agree modifications to Local Action Plans

How to do it: potential problems to be addressed

We now need to consider what possible mechanisms could be used to help achieve consensus. The basic aim in developing mechanisms is to ensure that all the stakeholders from service providers, local politicians and service user groups **meet on an equal basis**. This will always be the major constraint given that different groups are not of equal status in one another's eyes.

It is not possible to give detailed guidelines because the local institutional and political context determines what is workable. However, it is useful to identify the sorts of problems which are almost certain to arise. We can then try to make sure that these issues are taken into consideration in the actual mechanisms which are developed for consensus building in a particular place.

We do assume that the most likely mechanism will be based on some form of local committees and forums which will have representation from all stakeholders. This will include: the concerned Municipal Departments; specialist line agencies; Councillors and other local politicians; representatives of service user groups and other key target groups.

Table 3c.2. Potential problems faced by mechanisms for consensus building	
Problem to be addressed	**Description**
Vested/delegated authority	The Terms of Reference for a committee or forum for consensus building have to establish the authority which that group has to take decisions. The first exercise in consensus building may therefore be to obtain the consent of all parties that they will abide by the collective decision of the group. There are several approaches. ■ Authority is vested in the committee through the issuance of a Government Order; this implies high level support from regional or national government which is a pre-requisite if major changes to current operating procedures are envisaged. ■ The members of the committee voluntarily agree to accept the findings and rulings of the committee without recourse to enforcement. This means that the departments and line agencies agree to reflect the consensus decision in drawing up workplans and using their powers of administrative and technical sanction. This attitude is highly desirable even if the committee is supported by Government Order. ■ Delegation of financial powers; some governments, e.g. the State Government of Kerala in India, have opted for a truly decentralised approach which delegates financial authority to the local committee structure.
Leadership	Any activity which requires groups and agencies to be brought together, when they previously had no reason to talk to one another, requires strong, positive leadership. This individual needs to have: ■ sufficient authority within the town and within departments and agencies ■ respect of the various stakeholder groups involved ■ a commitment to progress, which may involve 'banging heads together'

Table 3c.2. (continued)

Problem to be addressed	Description
Incentives to participate	It is important to demonstrate that there will be tangible benefits to town services as a whole if departments and agencies are expected to alter their priorities and plans. ■ this needs high level agreement of both officials and councillors/local politicians who are also in a position to advocate the approach; otherwise nobody will listen ■ this is closely related to the leadership issue and the extent to which the approach is backed either by Government Order or through voluntary agreement ■ delegation of financial powers provides a compulsive incentive
Information sharing	A lot of information is required in order for members of committees, forums etc to make informed decisions on priorities; for example, everyone needs access to: ■ details of the proposals contained in the plans ■ Agency and Departmental workplans and investment proposals for the coming years ■ current priorities assigned by the concerned Departments and line agencies to particular network improvements through new works and improved O&M ■ most of this information is or should be in the public domain and there has to be a willingness to share it, particularly with representatives of user groups
Dispute resolution	Disputes arise when priorities are being discussed and defined and there need to be mechanisms for resolving these disputes. The spirit in which the committee or forum operates is critical; key issues include: ■ members from the different interest groups of service providers and service users have an equal voice; the main difficulty from past experience is that the views of the users are likely to be ignored ■ the possibility of appealing to a higher authority for arbitration on certain decisions; given the overall objective of consensus building, ideally this should be done informally by agreement rather than having to resort to statutory powers

Table 3c.2. continued	
Problem to be addressed	**Description**
Increased public awareness	Increasing general awareness and interest in service planning is an important wider role for consensus building. Public service agencies rarely make known to the general public what are the roles and responsibilities of different departments and organisations; the public tend to view 'the government' in general as being responsible for services. *Citizens guides* to particular services have been successfully used to create awareness of programmes and could be used to promote the positive things (for example, the Network Service Plans) which the town is doing on behalf of its residents.

How to do it: some examples

It is not possible to prescribe guaranteed ways or mechanisms for the process of consensus building. The following suggestions are based around the need to develop consensus at both the Ward and Municipal levels. The example described suggests:

- committees which have representation of the various stakeholder groups; and
- forums which are open to the general public; this could split down into a number of discussion groups around specific issues.

These link the different levels of planning: Local Action Plans are developed in a participatory way at the neighbourhood level: these then feed into the Ward level Area Network Services Plans; these in turn are coordinated at the municipal level.

There is experience of this approach in a number of places: in particular the state of Kerala in South India has pioneered a highly decentralised approach known as the Peoples' Planning Campaign from which many other states and governments could learn useful lessons. City forums facilitated by local NGOs have also been used in Karachi as a means of engendering more widespread ownership of important ideas related to city services.

The crucial point in any structure for consensus building is where the final authority for decision making actually lies, either with the committee, or the forum or with officials in line departments. This, and the actual roles and responsibilities, have to be worked out locally in the context of municipal, regional and national government policy and support.

Table 3c.3. Some suggestions for local structures

Structure	Possible Activities	Participation
Ward Committees	■ review the Area Network Service Plans ■ identify finance for improvements to O&M of local services ■ discussion of draft criteria for prioritising proposals in Area Network Service Plans ■ ensure that different local sources of finance are used in an optimum way to avoid piecemeal improvements i.e. ensure convergence of different sources of finance ■ review strategy for implementation of Area Network Service Plans ■ review workplans for new works and improved O&M ■ evaluate the likely impact of decisions on individual Local Action Plans and feedback the outcome to local user groups ■ negotiate Memorandum of Understanding for local Operation and Maintenance for each Local Action Plan (See Section 6)	■ representatives of the neighbourhoods including all those areas having Local Action Plans ■ locally elected leaders, Councillors and politicians ■ officials from municipal departments and line agencies ■ representatives of particular target groups e.g. women, poor, castes/tribes/ religions ■ representatives of other interest groups including the private sector

Table 3c.3. continued		
Structure	**Possible Activities**	**Participation**
Municipal Committee	■ review the co-ordinated plans for networked services at the town/city level ■ identify finance for new capital works ■ the Mayor may also have an important role in relation to councillor-based budgets, in that money needs to be brought back to the municipal centre in order to deal with 'lumpy' investments which benefit the city as a whole ■ identify finance for improvements to O&M of local services ■ discussion of draft criteria for prioritising proposals for networked services at the town/city level ■ review current institutional priorities of service providers ■ review strategy for implementation of Municipal Action Plan ■ review workplans for new works and improved O&M ■ evaluate the likely impact of decisions on Area Service Plans for each Ward	■ representatives chosen from the Ward Committees to include participants from the different groups. ■ senior officials from each municipal department ■ senior officials from both the Planning and Capital Works sections of line agencies ■ senior officials from the O&M section of line agencies

Table 3c.3. continued

Structure	Possible Activities	Participation
Ward Forum	Forum for presentation discussion and feedback to the Ward Committee of: ■ Area Network Service Plans ■ criteria for prioritising proposals for Area Network Service Plans ■ impact of priorities for Area Network Service Plans on Local Action Plans ■ implementation strategy ■ input to development of information such as 'citizens guides' to services operating from the Ward Offices ■ accountability of officials and politicians	■ open meeting for the general public ■ Ward Committee members
Town Forum	Forum for presentation discussion and feedback to the Municipal Committee of: ■ co-ordinated plans for networked services at the town/city level ■ criteria for prioritising proposals for co-ordinated plans for networked services at the town/city level ■ impact of priorities for co-ordinated plans for networked services at the town/city level on Area Service Plans ■ implementation strategy ■ input to development of information such as 'citizens guides' to central municipal services ■ accountability of officials and politicians	■ open meeting for the general public ■ Municipal Committee members

What if all this does not work?

We have to face the possibility, even the likelihood, that this complicated interlocking of local and municipal level planning will not work effectively. This will clearly have a major impact on the delivery of networked services and the extent to which the local improvements in the Local Action Plans can be implemented. We are then looking at local non-networked solutions which are by their nature limited in overall impact.

There are many successful examples of local initiatives; this is not in dispute. However, without bringing in the links with the wider infrastructure networks, many of the opportunities which are generated by peoples' action at the neighbourhood level will be lost.

See Tool 3 *The role of NGOs* for further information on the potential for and limitations of concerted local action.

www.ingramcontent.com/pod-product-compliance
Lightning Source LLC
Jackson TN
JSHW052008131224
75386JS00036B/1234